# FROM BOMBAY TO BRITAIN

SIGNATURE RECIPES FROM 50 OF THE UK'S FINEST INDIAN RESTAURANTS

First published in 2018 by RMC Media
6 Broadfield Court, Sheffield, S8 0XF
Tel: 0114 250 6300
www.rmcmedia.co.uk



Writer: Rhiana-Louise Hughes
Editor: Martin Edwards
Design & Typesetting: Steve Levers, Richard Abbey and Christopher Brierley
Photography: Tim Green and Matthew Horwood



Printed and bound in Malta by:
Gutenberg Press Ltd – www.gutenberg.com.mt
Gudja Road, Tarxien, Malta, GXQ 2902
Tel: 00356 2189 7037

A CIP catalogue record for this book is available from the British Library.

ISBN: 978-1-907998-36-2

This book is kindly sponsored by Kingfisher beer
in aid of *National Curry Week*

# CONTENTS



**THE RESTAURANTS**



**COLOUR KEY – UK REGIONS**

North East
North West
Yorshire And The Humber
East Midlands
West Midlands
London
South East
South West
Scotland
Wales

MOTHER INDIA
KITCHEN

# FOREWORD
## DIPNA ANAND

After years of involvement in the prestigious National Curry Week, I am pleased to be a part of this recipe book that not only showcases some of the UK's most-loved Indian restaurants, but also raises money for such an inspiring charity, Curry for Change. Using the nation's love of curry, all profits from this book will go towards vitally changing the lives of rural families in Asia and Africa who suffer from hunger. So don your apron, ramp up the heat, and get stuck in to any one of these 50 signature recipes – and don't forget to crack open a cool Kingfisher Beer!

*- Chef Dipna Anand*

# INDIA'S NUMBER ONE

**Kingfisher is India's number one, the first choice of the nation, from Delhi to Doddanapudi, and the leading Indian beer the world over.**

Brewed to an authentic and most venerable recipe for more than 150 years, it is the perfect partnership for the heat and spice of even the richest of curries.

Practice surely does make perfect.

## The History of Kingfisher Beer

Kingfisher is one of India's most heralded exports, with roots tracing all the way back to 1857, when Castle Breweries first started brewing in the majestic city of Mysore. In time, Castle Breweries joined forces with four competitors to form the company now proudly known as United Breweries.

Since this humble beginning, United Breweries has seen the fame and popularity of its beer spread, from Kerala in the south to Delhi in the north and everywhere in between. In the 1970s, Kingfisher triumphantly spread its wings into other countries and it can now be found across the world, including in the UK where it is brewed to the very same renowned recipe.

Wherever wonderful Indian cuisine is being served, Kingfisher won't be more than an arm's length away.

## National Curry Week

Kingfisher Beer's National Curry Week is a highly-anticipated event in the social calendar, running since 1998 and founded by the late Peter Grove who's vision was to celebrate the nation's favourite dish. Celebrated each October, it applauds the diverse culture in the UK and as a result of this, the many delicious dishes available to us on a daily basis.

As well as rejoicing in all things curry, National Curry Week's aim is to raise as much money as possible to fight malnourishment and poverty by supporting focussed charities working to feed the world's population. This year we are partnering with Curry for Change to support the life-changing work they carry out in Africa and Asia.

As part of the week-long celebrations, we've joined forces with some of the UK's top Indian restaurants to bring you a recipe book full of their signature dishes. So whether it's a classic Chicken Tikka Masala, or turning up the heat with a King Prawn Piro Piro, this book will get everyone's tastebuds tingling.

# CURRY FOR CHANGE

## WWW.CURRYFORCHANGE.ORG.UK

**National Curry Week's official charity campaign partner, Curry for Change, supports essential work across Africa and Asia to help vulnerable rural families to build a future free from poverty. This includes helping families to grow enough food so they don't go hungry, earn an income so they can provide for their families and access vital information on nutrition and health.**

To date the money raised by Curry for Change has totalled more than £198,000 – enough to change the lives of more than 19,800 families suffering from hunger. This year the campaign is bigger than ever before, thanks to their restaurant partners, cooking classes, chef ambassadors and generous sponsors like Kingfisher Beer.

## Meet the people Curry for Change is working alongside:

Together we can support women like Ramsheela to improve their crops and break the cycle of hunger and poverty.

*"Our village now has a savings group that meets every month. I took out a loan and bought seeds, farming equipment and hired labour to help me harvest my rice. This year I grew more rice than ever before, was able to pay back my loan and earn a profit".*

- Ramsheela, India.

Together we can support couples like Benson and Judith to trial new innovative farming techniques to improve their harvest. Through their hard work they increased their yield by 700% last year and now Benson shares his farming knowledge with 19 other local farmers to help them improve their farming techniques and combat hunger.

- Benson and Judith, Malawi.

Together we can help people like Edward to build skills and knowledge in order to earn an income.

*"I've learned about soil and water conservation techniques, as well as natural pest management. Now I grow pineapples, avocados, bananas, sweet potatoes, peas, cabbages, maize and finger millet with my wife. Half of what we produce we eat, the other half we sell".*

- Edward, Zimbabwe.

Together, we can support mothers like Alice to learn new farming techniques to grow enough food to feed her family. Alice has even made enough profit to set up a grocery store and hire help for her farm! Alice is proud of her achievements.

*"Before I would only be recognised for my poverty. Now I am recognised in my village because of the benefits the charity has bought. Now I can feed my whole family without any external support. Everything you can see here is coming from farming. It has taken just two years since we started. I have really made it".*

- Alice, Malawi

Curry for Change is the fundraising campaign run by linked charities Health Poverty Action and Find Your Feet. Registered Charity Number 290535.

# AAGRAH

## YORKSHIRE

**At 41 years old, Aagrah is no newcomer to the thriving Indian restaurant scene. It's impossible to dismiss Aagrah as just another Indian restaurant – it's Kashmiri cuisine they're known for, and what's more it has also been the foundation of a remarkable business success story.**

Aagrah's first restaurant was opened in Shipley in 1977, and since then they've added 11 more to their group across Yorkshire. A family-run business since its inception, each Aagrah restaurant is personally managed by a member of the family, and they take great care to ensure their ethos of introducing the 'spice of life' to customers' lives is consistently delivered. Being a family-run business, they feel that they are able to add more of a personal touch to their customers' experiences. As a result, it doesn't have that 'chain restaurant' feel about it.

Not bad for a restaurant that started out with a turnover of a measly £200. Less than a decade later there were five restaurants turning over nearly £2million. And the story of Mohammed Aslam's business career was going only one way – and that was upwards.

While they do use their authentic family recipes in their restaurants, they're constantly developing these as well as adding new, innovative dishes to their menu.

The majority of Aagrah's restaurants are village based, so they have a strong and loyal local customer base behind them. Aagrah were this year's winner of Best Asian Restaurant Chain in the North of England at the Asian Restaurant Awards, and they have a long history of receiving awards, proof that the high quality of food and service that we can expect from them today is something that has been there from the start.

**Find them at:**

Chapel Allerton, Leeds City, Tadcaster, Shipley, Midpoint, Garforth, Skipton, Wakefield, Doncaster, Sheffield, Crystal Peaks

**www.aagrah.com**

# MURGH HYDERABADI

**Serves 4**

**INGREDIENTS**

1 medium cinnamon stick
2 black cardamom seeds
12g coriander seeds
6g cumin seeds
6g black cumin seeds
12g poppy seeds
6 black peppercorns
5 cloves
6g fenugreek leaves
3 bay leaves
50ml vegetable oil
2 medium onions, chopped
50g garlic purée
5 medium tomatoes, cut into four
50ml double cream
60ml natural yoghurt
12g red chilli powder
9g turmeric powder
12g salt
1kg boneless chicken, cubed
4 green chillies, chopped
5 leaves fresh coriander, cut into strips
10ml kewra water

**This authentic Sindhi-style Korma is far and away the most popular dish in the Aagrah restaurants due to its exceptional flavour and extensive use of spices. Aagrah adapted the original recipe for their menu and the dish is among those that won the Aagrah director, Mohammed Aslam, the International Chef of the Year award.**

Grind together the cinnamon stick, cardamom, coriander, cumin, black cumin, and poppy seeds, black peppercorns, cloves, fenugreek and bay leaves.

Heat the oil in a pan and half fry the onions, adding a splash of water to make sure they don't burn.

Add the garlic, ginger, tomatoes, double cream and yoghurt to the pan and cook for 10 minutes on a medium heat.

Add the ground spices and cook for a further 5 minutes on a low heat, adding a splash of water to avoid burning the spices.

Add red chilli powder, turmeric powder and salt and cook for 15 minutes until the oil begins to separate from the sauce.

Add the chicken to the sauce and stir frequently until cooked through.

Add the green chilli, fresh coriander and kewra water and cook for a further few minutes.

Serve.

## THE AMBRETTE

# PAV BHAJI

**Serves 4**

**INGREDIENTS**

500g potatoes
100ml vegetable oil
4 green chillies, deseeded and chopped
1 tablespoon ginger, finely chopped
250g tomatoes, chopped
4 whole red chillies, ground
1 teaspoon garlic paste
1 teaspoon ginger paste
75g butter
2 teaspoon garam masala
1 tablespoon fresh coriander, chopped
1 tablespoon lemon juice
4 soft white buns
Salt, to taste

**This dish originated in the 1850s as a fast lunchtime dish for textile workers in Mumbai. It rose to fame on the streets of the city, which was known for its street food culture. The simple potato and tomato dish has grown to have universal appeal, in spite of it originally being created as a poor man's meal.**

Peel and dice the potatoes, boil until soft and then set aside.

Heat oil in a large, heavy-based, flat pan.

Add the green chillies, fresh chopped ginger and tomatoes.

Sauté over a medium heat for three minutes, then add the red chillies and potatoes.

Reduce to a low heat, then stir fry and mash at the same time using a metal spatula.

Dissolve the ginger and garlic pastes in 100ml of water and sprinkle over the dish while stirring.

Adjust the seasoning to your taste, then increase to a medium heat and add the butter.

Sprinkle the garam masala, fresh coriander and lemon juice over the dish.

Apply butter onto the buns and grill until they turn a golden brown.

Serve the buns steaming hot with the bhaji.

# THE AMBRETTE
## MARGATE, CANTERBURY, RYE

**The first thing to strike you about this restaurant is the name. If you had to hazard a guess, you might think it was a French eatery. It's easy to visualise early evening promenaders out for a bracing stroll along the Margate shore, working up an appetite for moules mariniere at The Ambrette. Or perhaps it could be a type of Italian motor scooter favoured by mods on the lookout for their sworn leather-clad biker enemies on the seafront.**

None of these is near the mark. An Ambrette is actually a tropical plant renowned for its medicinal properties and aromatic qualities. Hence the fact that its namesake is a restaurant taking a fresh and modern approach to Indian cuisine.

Dev and Emma Biswal opened The Ambrette in February 2010, with the aim of challenging the status quo and bringing something new and exciting to the people of Kent. With Dev developing the overall concept behind The Ambrette and Emma looking after the back office side of things, the two have managed to grow into a three restaurant business, with customers flocking to their Margate, Rye and Canterbury locations.

The menu at The Ambrette focuses on regional Indian dishes, and their menus evolve with the seasons as new and fresh produce become available in the markets. Inspired by the local richness and variety, The Ambrette's menu features ingredients such as wood pigeon, quail and seafood, all sourced from within the UK.

They also stay true to many Indian staples. Their menus feature dhokla from Gujarat, dosas from Tamil Nadu and tandoori style dishes from Punjab, and they host regional food festivals highlighting Goan, Rajasthani and Kerala cuisines among others, featuring taster dishes from each region for their customers to try.

Through the hard work they've put into their restaurants, the Biswals and their team aspire to make people consider Indian cooking as on par with other world cuisines, such as French and Japanese. They want customers to know that Indian food is now much more than just a curry. It seems that they're achieving this, as customers visit them from

across the UK and they've earned themselves large groups of strongly supportive local diners.

In the years to come, Dev and Emma hope to open more restaurants in the South East, and continue to increase awareness about the diversity and variety that there is in Indian cooking, that isn't always shown to the UK consumer.

**Find them at:**

Margate Sea Front, 10 Fort Hill, Margate, CT9 1HD
Tel: 01843 231504
Email: margate@theambrette.co.uk

14-15 Beer Cart Lane, Canterbury, Kent, CT1 2NY
Tel: 01227 200777
Email: canterbury@theambrette.co.uk

The Devil in Rye
6 High Street, Rye, East Sussex, TN31 7JE
Tel: 07377 562625
Email: info@thedevilinrye.co.uk
**www.theambrette.co.uk**

# ASHOKA
## SHEFFIELD

**"Never knowingly underspiced".**

Next time you're in Sheffield, take a quick glance at the roadside signs on the roundabouts or dual carriageway. (Don't take too long about it, as accidents can be expensive and bad for your health).

You'll see a clever slogan like the above, and also others in a parody of the Sheffield accent – "Reyt good curreh" for instance.

They're the work of Rahul Amin, owner of the Ashoka Restaurant on the city's lively Ecclesall Road. And even the advertising standards people certainly wouldn't disagree, for the curry there is, by any standards, reyt good.

The youthful Rahul took over at the Ashoka 14 years ago. In doing so, he became only the second owner since 1967. The restaurant is a legend in the city, as was its previous proprietor, the late Kamal Ahmed.

The smallish, 36-seat Ashoka restaurant has a central aisle running the length of it. It was on this thoroughfare that Kamal would pace up and down the restaurant, checking on proceedings at each table in turn. It was well-established wisdom not to engage him in conversation. Not unless you had no plans for the next three hours.

But Rahul is his own man, and set about transforming the place practically as soon as he had the keys.

The result is spectacular, and so is his menu. Ashoka are

'inspired by India – made in Sheffield', and they're continuously adding new dishes and removing others from their menu to keep things interesting. They've got dishes for everyone, whether you can handle the spice or you like to live life on the mild side. Their Taxi Driver Curry is a favourite of their more daring diners, while dishes such as their Matar Paneer or Ginger Brinjal can be enjoyed by all.

Ashoka's menu isn't region specific, so whether it's from the shores of Kerala or the Hill Stations like Ooty, if it tastes delicious they'll put it on the menu.

**Find them at:**
307 Ecclesall Road, Sheffield, S11 8NX
Tel: 0114 268 3029
**www.ashoka1967.com**

# HENDERSONS HOUSE PURI

**Serves 4**

**INGREDIENTS**

**FOR THE PURI**

40g plain flour
½ teaspoon salt
Water
Vegetable oil for deep frying

**FOR THE FILLING**

Large handful baby potatoes
1 white onion, halved and thinly sliced
3 cloves garlic, finely chopped
¼ teaspoon chilli powder
½ teaspoon garam masala powder
¼ teaspoon turmeric powder
¼ can chickpeas
1 lemon
Salt, to taste
Hendersons relish
Coriander, chopped, to serve

**Hendersons is intrinsically linked to India with its exotic flavours derived from tamarind, cayenne, garlic and cloves. Ashoka have been using Hendersons in their House Puri for over four decades, and it's remained a favourite with diners all this time.**

Combine the flour and salt in a large mixing bowl, adding the water slowly to make a medium-firm dough.

Cover with clingfilm and leave in the fridge for 20 minutes.

Add plenty of flour to your rolling pin and board, shape the dough into ping-pong-sized balls and then roll out into flat discs.

Heat the oil for frying, remove any excess flour from the rolled bread and place into the oil.

Using a metal spatula, as the puri is frying, skim the surface of the oil and splash onto the puri as it rises, then once cooked set the puri aside.

Wash and cut the baby potatoes into 1cm cubes.

Heat two tablespoons of vegetable oil in a large pan and gently fry the potatoes and onions for a few minutes.

Add the garlic, chilli powder, garam masala powder and turmeric powder and cook on a medium heat for a further 10 minutes, stirring frequently.

Add the chickpeas, juice of half a lemon and salt to taste, then add the Hendersons relish to taste (Ashoka usually add a fair few splashes)

Crack the top of the puri and place the filling inside, garnish with chopped coriander and serve.

# SHRIMP KHICHRI WITH TANDOORI SPICED LOBSTER

## SERVED WITH SAUTÉED SPINACH AND WILD MUSHROOMS

**Serves 4**

**INGREDIENTS**

**SHRIMP KHICHRI**

200g split yellow mung beans
1 litre white fish stock (or water)
Pinch ground turmeric
75g ghee (or clarified butter)
1 teaspoon royal cumin seeds
2 onions, chopped
1 inch piece fresh ginger, finely chopped
4 Indian green chillies, finely chopped
Salt, to taste
100g raw prawns/shrimps, shelled
2 tomatoes, deseeded and cut into half-inch pieces
1 teaspoon dry shrimp paste
150g cooked basmati rice
Juice of 1 lemon
2 tablespoons fresh coriander, chopped

**LOBSTER MARINADE**

75g ginger and garlic paste
1 tablespoon Kashmiri chilli powder
1 tablespoon Bengali mustard oil*
1 teaspoon garam masala
Juice of half a lemon
Salt, to taste
4 lobster tails

**GARNISH**

5g baby spinach
150g wild mushrooms
4 Sabudana poppadum

**Available from your local Asian supermarket or specialist food shop*

**Inspired by home cooking and childhood memories, this dish is a combination of seafood khichri with wild mushrooms, shellfish and poppadum, and can be found in almost every state in India. A dish that can be enjoyed all year round, it's a fairly new addition to the menu at Baluchi but it's already proving popular with guests who can almost taste the sense of nostalgia that the dish brings to the restaurant's chefs.**

Pre-heat oven to 170°C.

Prepare the marinade for the lobster tails by combining all marinade ingredients (except tails) in a small bowl.

Heat a large pan of water and when it begins to boil, add the lobster tails and boil for 6 minutes.

While the lobster is boiling, get a large bowl of ice-cold water ready. As soon as the tails are cooked, remove with tongs and plunge into the cold water.

Remove them from the water, place on kitchen roll and pat dry.

Once dry, coat the lobster tails in the marinade.

Place the lobster tails in the pre-heated oven and cook for 8 minutes.

To make the shrimp Khichri, first rinse the mung beans, then put them in a saucepan with fish stock (or water) and turmeric and bring to boil.

Simmer until the beans are cooked and tender, then mix in the remaining water. Remove from heat and set aside.

Heat 60g of ghee (or butter) in a heavy pan and add the cumin seeds. When they begin to crackle, add the onions and sauté until they start to turn golden brown.

Add the ginger, green chillies and salt and sauté for a further minute.

Add the prawns and cook for 2-3 minutes.

Stir in the mung beans and bring to boil.

Add tomatoes and shrimp paste and cook for another 2-3 minutes, then fold in the rice.

Mix carefully, enough to heat the rice through, taking care not to break it up.

Place the rice on a plate with the lobster tail and finish the dish by melting the remaining ghee and drizzling it over the rice.

Sprinkle the lemon juice and coriander on top.

Serve immediately with sautéed spinach and wild mushrooms with butter and salt.

# BALUCHI

## LONDON

**As back-to-school experiences go, this has to be one of the best. Set within the Great Hall of the 120-year-old neo-baroque building that was once St Olave's Grammar School, Baluchi's home is part of The LaLiT London, the only UK hotel in the five-star Indian chain.**

Each room within the hotel is ornamented with bespoke Indian art, with the result that Indian culture and British charm are seamlessly combined throughout. Witness the ever-popular afternoon tea (with an Indian twist), while the menu proper is inspired by the rich curries of the north-west frontier.

First-time visitors are often left speechless as they enter the Great Hall. Vaulted ceilings and large windows allow natural light to fill the room, while the Hyderabadi hand-crafted glass chandeliers and the pops of deep cobalt found across the room really warm the space, and make it clear that you are about to dine in an authentically Indian restaurant.

The menu features traditional dishes from Kashmir, Bengal, Kerala, Goa and more, and pairs the complex and historical flavours of Indian cuisine with the finest international culinary concepts of today.

The menu at Baluchi offers a six-course tasting feast as well as a six-course vegetarian tasting menu, both with perfectly paired wine flights to accompany them. Baluchi is open seven days a week and has a menu varied enough that you could come back each day and try something new. With 14 different breads available from The Naan'ery – the restaurant's clever take on a bakery, where artisan breads are prepared in a specially made cast-iron tandoor. One thing's for sure, you'll never be short on accompaniments.

Baluchi's desserts are another good reason to visit the restaurant. The dessert menu contains the intriguing-sounding saffron-infused compressed pineapple, served with a cardamom ice-cream and pink peppercorn tuille, or perhaps curry smoke flavoured coconut (part of their Coconut Three Ways dessert).

**Find them at:**

The LaLiT London, 181 Tooley Street, London, SE1 2JR

Tel: 020 3765 0000

Email: london@thelalit.com

**www.thebaluchi.com**

# BOMBAY BRASSERIE
## LONDON

**Bombay, now known as Mumbai, was and still is a cultural melting pot, bringing together people from all over India, Asia and the rest of the world. This is of course reflected in the food, and the Bombay Brasserie is by general acclaim the standard bearer for this eclectic style.**

It was not always so. Despite being part of the world-renowned Taj group of hotels, Bombay Brasserie opened to a somewhat mixed reception in December 1982. Although the restaurant nailed its colours to the mast with an authentic menu, UK customers found it unfamiliar territory at the time, when new textures and flavours were presented to them. As the years have passed, the restaurant has grown from 100 seats to over 220, a clear indication of how things have changed and demand has risen.

Bombay Brasserie believe that until they opened their doors, Indian food being served in the UK was not a true reflection of the old country's cuisine. Restaurants on these shores were generalising the food that they served, offering dishes with spice levels ranging from korma for mild and vindaloo for hot. They realised the food in India had more nuances of flavour and that eating it was more of a communal experience, every meal being an occasion to share with family and friends. And this is exactly what they have brought over to London.

The Proud Recipient of a Lifetime Achievement Award from The Good Curry Guide, executive chef Prahlad Hedge is credited as being one of the reasons the restaurant is so popular today. Hedge prepares all of his own spices to ensure flavours and textures are perfectly extracted and placed in each dish. Working together with chef Sriram Aylur, founder of Michelin-starred Quilon, they strive to ensure each dish exceeds expectations. The large dishes are perfect for sharing with friends, family or colleagues.

**Find them at:**
Courtfield Road, London, SW7 4QH
Tel: 020 7370 4040
Email: dine@bombayb.co.uk
**www.bombayb.co.uk**

# MASALA SEABASS

**Serves 1**

**INGREDIENTS**

3g chilli powder
3g turmeric powder
Salt, to taste
20ml lime juice
180g Chilean seabass, de-boned and skin-on
20ml oil
3g cumin
5g garlic, chopped
80g mushrooms, sliced
200g baby spinach, shredded
Salt, to taste

**GARNISH**

1 chilli flower
1 chive
1 lime wedge
Few drops chilli oil

**Derived from a simple pan-fried fish dish cooked throughout various regions of India, Bombay Brasserie use simple and easy to find ingredients to create this popular dish. The team of chefs use Chilean seabass in favour of other proteins as they have found it has a great taste and texture on its own, one which is even further elevated when combined with the spinach and mushroom base. Easy to put together, this dish is a great – and much healthier – alternative to your Friday or Saturday night takeaway!**

Preheat the oven to 180°C.

Apply chilli and turmeric powders, salt and lime juice to the sea bass and leave to marinate for 20 minutes.

Heat the oil in a pan and sear the marinated sea bass on both sides.

Place the sea bass on a baking tray and place in the oven for 5 minutes.

While the sea bass is cooking, heat oil in a pan, add the cumin and chopped garlic and sauté.

Add in the sliced mushrooms and shredded spinach, stir-fry until cooked.

Add salt to taste.

**To serve**

Assemble the spinach and mushroom base in the centre of a plate and top with the sea bass (skin side up).

Arrange the chilli flower, chive and lime wedge on top of the fish.

Drizzle a few drops of chilli oil around the plate and serve.

# TANDOORI JHINGA

**Serves 1**

**INGREDIENTS**

1 teaspoon cardamom seeds
1 teaspoon black peppercorns
1 teaspoon black cumin seeds
1 teaspoon whole cloves
Third of a whole nutmeg
Medium cinnamon stick, broken into 3-4 pieces

**GARNISH**

Fresh lime juice
Fresh coriander, chopped

**Available at your local Indian/Asian supermarket*

**Fresh tiger prawns marinated overnight with spices, ginger, garlic and yoghurt, grilled to perfection! This dish requires overnight preparation, so make sure you allow yourself plenty of time!**

Place all garam masala ingredients into a pestle and mortar and grind down to a powder, then set aside.

Devein the prawns but keep the tails (make sure that the black vein is completely removed from head to tail).

Wash the prawns thoroughly and strain to remove water.

Put the prawns on a dry cloth to remove any excess moisture.

Place the prawns in a bowl and add all of the ingredients except the yoghurt and Kashmiri masala.

Mix well and leave for 20 minutes to marinate in the spices.

In a bowl, combine the yoghurt and Kashmiri masala to make a paste (you can add some yellow food colouring for an extra pop of colour).

Mix the marinated prawns with the paste.

Add the mustard oil, mix again and leave to refrigerate overnight.

Once the prawns have been chilled overnight, bake on either a robata grill or a barbecue for best results (you can grill in the oven if you do not have these available).

While grilling, baste the prawns with ghee or oil to add a smoky flavour to the prawns.

# BOMBAY PALACE

## LONDON

**Part of an international chain of Indian restaurants with locations in Asia and North America, the UK branch of Bombay Palace opened in 1981 in swanky central London. Serving food inspired mainly by the North-West Indian region of Punjab, Bombay Palace has remained true to authentic Indian cuisine and has not followed the trend of adding experimental fusion dishes to their menu – despite some temptation!**

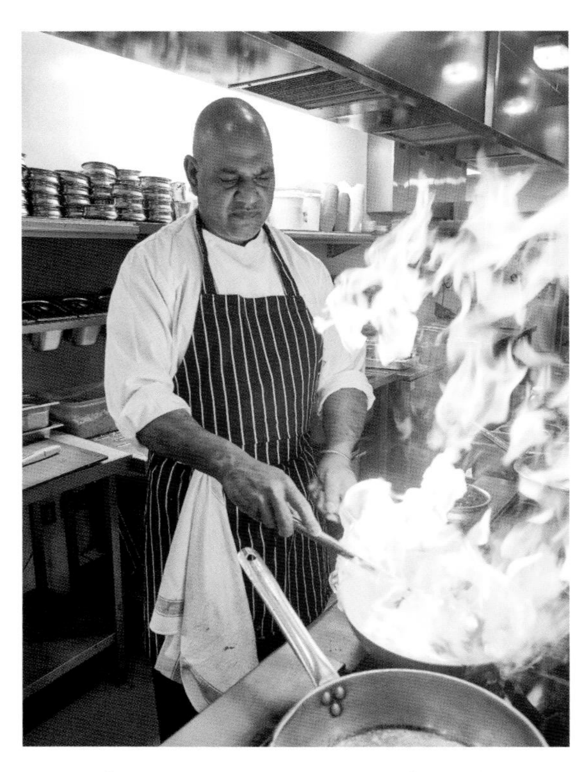

The man behind Bombay Palace chain is Sant Singh Chatwal. While today he calls New York home, Sant grew up in Punjab, a region known for its colourful cuisine. He wanted to change the perception of Indian restaurants across the world from being just your average curry house to fine dining establishments serving elegant, sophisticated cuisine. Not wanting to follow the crowd, Sant has ensured that Bombay Palace remains just one of the few fine-dining Indian restaurants in London to continue serving only the most authentic and traditional Indian cuisine.

In the early days Sant had a mission to change the way people saw Indian dining, and while it has taken a long time for this to happen, UK diners today seem to be more comfortable with real Indian cuisine. Exciting young chefs full of ideas have inspired a sea change in the way Indian food is perceived by diners, putting their own unique twists on decades old recipes.

Knowing that Indian cuisine, especially that in London, has changed for the better over recent years, Sant and all the team are confident that one day they will achieve their goal of opening a Bombay Palace restaurant in every major city across the globe.

**Find them at:**
50 Connaught Street, London, W2 2AA
Tel: 020 7723 8855
Email: info@bombay-palace.co.uk
**www.bombay-palace.co.uk**

# THE BRILLIANT RESTAURANT

## MIDDLESEX

**Its visitor list includes everyone from Prime Minister Ted Heath to Prince Charles. But don't get the idea that this is the retreat of celebrities, footballers and the super-rich. It's a very good, down-to-earth authentic Indian restaurant where the dishes will be familiar to curry lovers.**

Since 1975, the team at The Brilliant have been serving food inspired by North Indian cuisine, along with their late grandfather's recipes. And it's something they do exceptionally well, with the result that its fame has spread far beyond its home in Southall, Middlesex. The Anand family have been running the business for three generations – and have three generations of loyal customers supporting them.

Today, The Brilliant is run by Gulu Anand alongside his daughter Dipna, and son Shanker. They still see many customers coming to dine with them who used to frequent their grandfather's restaurant in Kenya during the 1950s and 60s. And this generation naturally bring with them their own children and grandchildren.

Since it first opened, The Brilliant has been extended seven times and grown from a 36-seat restaurant to one which can lay claim to more than 275. The Anands have continued to expand their Southall location instead of opening up new branches as their experience shows that customers will continue to travel to them.

It's a formula that has certainly proved to be sound. Having been featured on Gordon Ramsay's Best Restaurant TV series, the Anand family are no strangers to receiving recognition and achieving success. They have opened up their own Brilliant School of Cookery, published their own, splendidly-illustrated cookbook, Beyond Brilliant, not to mention sealing catering contracts with both the Wembley SSE Arena and the O2. And the book proved to be a sell-out, with another few thousand copies being ordered to meet continuing demand.

Enough to be going on with? Not quite. They have recently opened Dip in Brilliant in Fulham, with Dipna at the helm, and hope in the future to open up further branches.

**Find them at:**

72-76 Western Road, Southall, Middlesex, UB2 5DZ

Tel: 020 8574 1928

Email: info@brilliantrestaurant.com

**www.brilliantrestaurant.com**

# OH MY COD

## FISH AND CHIPS WITH A DESI SWERVE

**Serves 4-5**

**INGREDIENTS**

**FISH**

360g plain flour
400-420ml Kingfisher Beer*
2 teaspoons salt
4 or 5 x 175g cod fillets, skinned and boned
Sunflower oil for deep frying
¾ teaspoon black pepper powder
1 ½ teaspoons red chilli powder
1 teaspoon garam masala

**TARTARE SAUCE**

260g mayonnaise
70g gherkins, finely chopped
30g capers, finely chopped
Pinch salt
Pinch black pepper powder
¼ teaspoon chaat masala

**CHIPS**

1kg Maris Piper, King Edward or Desiree potatoes
Sunflower oil, for deep frying
Pinch of salt

**MUSHY PEAS**

450g peas, tinned or frozen
1 ½ tablespoons double cream
20g butter, melted
¾ teaspoon salt
¼ teaspoon black pepper powder
1 tablespoon fresh coriander, chopped
1 teaspoon cumin seeds

**If you would prefer not to use beer for the fish batter, sparkling water is a great alternative, add ¼ teaspoon baking powder and 1 egg and leave in the fridge for 20 minutes before using.*

Takeaways are a Friday night treat across the UK, but how do you decide between popping down to your local chippy or spicing up your evening with an Indian? This dish allows you to combine the two – without having to sit and wait for the delivery man to ring your doorbell! Having tried and tested numerous different recipes, the team at the Brilliant restaurant found that beer aids in producing the crunchiest and fluffiest of batters and the touch of masala works beautifully with the cod fish. Add some home-made chips, spiced tartare sauce and some cumin infused mushy peas and you'll never have to dig through 'that drawer' to find your favourite takeaway menu again.

### Fish

Pre-heat the oven to 150°C and the oil to 180°C for deep frying.
Whisk together 280g of the flour, beer (or sparkling water), and remaining ingredients until smooth and leave to rest for 15 minutes.
Make sure the fish is dry and dust lightly with the remaining flour.
Dip the fish into the batter until coated well all over, then carefully place in the hot oil and cook for 6-8 minutes until golden and crispy.
Remove from the pan/fryer, drain and sit on a baking tray lined with greaseproof paper.
Place in the pre-heated oven to keep warm while you prepare the remaining fillets.

### Chips

Peel the potatoes and cut into your preferred size, then rinse well in cold water.
Parboil the chips in boiling salted water for 4-5 minutes until softened but still retaining their shape.
Drain and pat dry, then deep fry in oil for 7-8 minutes or until golden and crisp.

### Mushy Peas

Bring a shallow pot of water to the boil over a medium-high heat.
Add the peas and cook for 3 minutes until tender, then drain and transfer to a blender or food processor.
Dry-roast the cumin seeds in a pan for 2-3 minutes.
Add the remaining ingredients and process until blended but still thick with small pieces of peas.

### Tartare Sauce

Mix together all ingredients.
Adjust seasoning to taste and serve with the fish, chips and mushy peas.

# CHICKEN TIKKA MASALA

**Serves 2**

INGREDIENTS

SAUCE

350g tinned chopped tomatoes
1 teaspoon fresh ginger
2 cloves garlic
2 tablespoon vegetable oil
Salt, to taste
1 teaspoon cinnamon powder
1 teaspoon cardamom powder
½ teaspoon red Kashmiri chilli powder
½ green chilli
½ teaspoon coriander powder
½ teaspoon cumin powder
1 teaspoon garam masala
1 teaspoon dried fenugreek leaves
½ teaspoon turmeric powder
1 teaspoon sugar
1 tablespoon honey
2 tablespoons butter
4 tablespoons double cream

MARINADE

200g diced chicken breast
1½ teaspoons red Kashmiri chilli powder
1 teaspoon turmeric powder
1 teaspoon garam masala
1 teaspoon dried fenugreek leaves
1 teaspoon salt
1 tablespoon yoghurt

Preheat the oven to 180°C.

Combine the ingredients for the marinade in a large bowl and marinate the chicken for 10 minutes.

Place the chicken in the pre-heated oven and cook for 15 minutes.

Blend the tomatoes to make a smooth tomato purée and set aside.

Blend together the ginger and garlic to make a paste.

Heat the oil in a pan and when hot, add the ginger and garlic paste and sauté for 1 minute.

Add the tomato purée and cook for a further 3 minutes.

MATCHES
the

# THE CAT'S PYJAMAS

## LEEDS, YORK

**It's been just three years since The Cat's Pyjamas opened its first restaurant in the Leeds suburb of Headingley. Running a research company specialising in food and drink meant that owner Alison White was aware of the gap in the market for a uniquely authentic Indian restaurant. And when her landlord informed her that the unit downstairs was soon to be available, she gave herself no choice but to snap up the opportunity at hand.**

Confident that they serve 'the best Indian street food this side of Delhi', The Cat's Pyjamas pride themselves on the authenticity of their food. Before the restaurant opened, Alison spent months researching authentic Indian cuisine and craft beer, working closely with Alfred Prasad, the youngest Indian chef to ever receive a Michelin star. Each dish here is prepared by chefs who grew up eating the dishes they now make for their customers, and with the help of head chef Daljit Singh, the menu continues to grow and develop.

The menu at The Cat's Pyjamas is inspired by the local dishes of India's hawkers, Goa's seafood shacks and the toddy shops of Kerala, each dish infused with the passion of India's cooks. Customer favourites include the Kolkata Chaat and the Punjabi Chole, and each can be paired with some of The Cat's Pyjamas' favourite craft beers.

The energy from the restaurant's bustling kitchen spills over into the dining area where you see the vibrant décor evoke the colours and the chaos of India, yet still manage to create an easy-going atmosphere. It's a formula that seems to be working – Alison has just opened her third independent restaurant in York with further branches due to open in Wakefield, Sheffield and Harrogate by the end of the year.

**Find them at:**

53 Otley Road, Headingley, Leeds, LS6 3AB
Tel: 0113 274 2618
Email: headingley@thecatspjs.co.uk

9 Eastgate, Leeds, LS2 7LY
Tel: 0113 234 0454
Email: eastgate@thecatspjs.co.uk

2 Cumberland Street, York, YO1 9SW
Tel: 01904 530220
Email: york@thecatspjs.co.uk
**www.thecatspjs.co.uk**

# CHAAKOO
## GLASGOW

**Chaakoo's first goal was to be embraced by the food lovers of Glasgow and within ten weeks of opening they held the top spot on tripadvisor above the other 2,000 restaurants in the city.**

They've remained in the top 20 ever since, proving they were and still are, accepted wholeheartedly. Chaakoo is a restaurant that through its menu encourages its guests to try something new and to treat dining out as a shared experience, rather than just one of necessity.

Paul Sloan, the man behind Chaakoo, has spent his life travelling the world and believes that in classic curry houses, guests tend to stick with what they know. By having a menu made up of small plates, Chaakoo's diners are able to pick two or three dishes – or more, they're not judgemental – and try something new, as well as sticking by their go-to dish if they still feel they need something familiar to fall back on. The small plates allow families or groups of friends to each order something different and share it amongst themselves.

At Chaakoo, the menu is inspired by the experiences of the chefs. They've avoided anglicising their dishes and they make sure that each one is prepared just as it would be in India and that guests are having a genuine experience with authentic Indian cuisine.

Believing that they're only as good as their last customer's experience, Chaakoo work tirelessly to provide their diners with the best experience possible. They take pride in their team, and they do their best to ensure that each member of staff is enjoying their job, as when the team has fun, their guests do too.

They've won accolades and awards, but their main goal will always be to ensure that everyone who dines with them leaves with full bellies and high spirits.

**Find them at:**
79 St Vincent Street, Glasgow, G2 5TF
Tel: 0141 229 0000
Email: stvincent@chaakoo.co.uk
**www.chaakoo.co.uk**

# CHICKEN DHANSAK

**Serves 4**

**INGREDIENTS**
300ml rapeseed oil
15g cumin seeds
6 green cardamom pods
6 cloves
10 black peppercorns
4 black cardamom pods
2 medium onions, diced
3 green chillies, chopped
1 tablespoon ginger, chopped
1 tablespoon garlic, chopped
1 tablespoon turmeric powder
1 tablespoon red chilli powder
1 tablespoon dried coriander
3 medium tomatoes, diced
300g chana daal (soaked overnight)
1 litre water
1kg chicken, cut into 2-inch pieces
½ bunch fenugreek leaves
½ bunch coriander

**Chaakoo are inspired by the original cafés that were widespread in Mumbai during the 1950s. Now, very few original cafés are left, and Chaakoo wanted to recreate their spirit of inclusivity and great food in Glasgow. The Dhansak is an old dish that was a result of the interactions between Indians and immigrants, combining Persian and Gujarati cuisine. In India, the dish is often cooked for a whole day, which echoes the time they take when preparing their own curries at Chaakoo. The trick is not to rush the Dhansak, leaving time for the flavours to mingle after you've taken it off the heat.**

Heat the oil in a pan. Add cumin seeds, green cardamom, cloves, black peppercorns and black cardamom and stir well for 2 minutes.

Add the onions and the green chillies and sauté until the onions soften and turn golden brown.

Add the chopped ginger and garlic and stir for 1 minute.

Add the turmeric powder, red chilli powder and the dried coriander and stir.

Add the tomatoes and stir, bringing the sauce to a simmer.

Add the chana daal and 1 litre of water, bring to a boil then reduce to a simmer and cover, leave to cook for 20 minutes.

Uncover the pan, add the chicken and the fenugreek leaves and cook for another 20 minutes.

Take off the heat, stir through the fresh coriander leaves, cover and leave to stand for 10 minutes.

Serve.

# RAJASTHANI LAAL MAAS

**Serves 4**

**INGREDIENTS**

245g yoghurt
2 tablespoons ginger and garlic paste
3 tablespoons Mathania chilli paste or Kashmiri chilli paste*
1 tablespoon coriander powder
½ teaspoon turmeric powder
½ tablespoon cumin powder
4 tablespoons ghee
1 tablespoon cold pressed mustard oil
3cm cinnamon stick
3 cloves
1 black cardamom
500g onions, thinly sliced
Salt, to taste
500g lamb leg, diced
Red chillies, to garnish

**To make your own chilli paste, soak 10-12 whole red chillies in hot water for 30 minutes, drain the water and grind the chillies to a fine paste. Add water while grinding the chillies to achieve a smooth and thick consistency.*

A lamb curry hailing from Rajasthan, this dish is typically very hot and rich in chillies and garlic. Traditionally made with wild game meat such as boar or deer, the dish was a favourite among the royal families. While the level of spice remains the same today, the meat used in the dish is usually tender mutton or lamb. Chapatis or bajra are both great accompaniments.

Add the yoghurt, ginger and garlic paste, chilli paste, coriander powder, turmeric powder and cumin powder to a bowl, mix well and set aside.

Heat the ghee and mustard oil in a saucepan and add the cinnamon, cloves and black cardamom.

Add the sliced onions and salt and cook until golden brown.

Add the lamb and toss well with the onions until the lamb is seared.

Add the yoghurt mix and stir for a further 5 minutes.

Add some water and mix well.

Cover the pan and simmer for 30-40 minutes, until the lamb is tender.

Remove and place into a serving dish and garnish with whole red chillies.

# CHAI NAASTO

## BECKENHAM, LONDON, HARROW

**Brothers Tilesh, Viren and Nimesh Solanki were inspired to open Chai Naasto as an homage to their grandmother, or Nani, as they call her. The brothers used to visit their Nani over their school summer holidays and would always look forward to the food she'd make them. As they got older, they started taking Nani's cooking to work and even found that people were willing to buy it from them. This was when they realised that they could turn the food they've always known and loved into a business.**

Born in Mogadishu, Somalia to Indian parents, Nani began cooking at the age of ten and throughout her life has travelled across the world learning about different cuisines, implementing what she has seen and experienced into her own cooking. To this day, Nani makes all of her own spices, and it's these that are used in the Chai Naasto restaurants.

It was a brave move, since none of the three Solanki brothers had any experience at all in the restaurant industry. But the trio – a Heathrow worker, MOT garage owner and IT lecturer – took Nani's advice and threw all that they had into Chai Naasto, and clearly the risk has paid off as they are now the owners of three Chai Naasto restaurants. Even though they've expanded their business, they still ensure that every customer that comes to dine with them feels as though they're walking into their Nani's home.

Family is at the core of everything that they do at Chai Naasto, and while they do use Nani's spices at their restaurants, the brothers have put a modern twist on her dishes and make sure that their menu never appears outdated. Every two to three months they choose a new state to inspire their menu. They've taken their customers on journeys through Punjab, Hyderabad and Gujarat to name but a few, and this September they launched their new menu in collaboration with MasterChef runner up Nisha Parmar.

**Find them at:**

2-4 Fairfield Road, Beckenham, BR3 3LD
Tel: 020 3750 0888
Email: beckenham@chai-naasto.co.uk

103 Hammersmith Grove, London, W6 0NQ
Tel: 020 8741 1088
Email: hammersmith@chai-naasto.co.uk

242 Streatfield Road, Harrow, HA3 9BX
Tel: 020 8204 4660
Email: harrow@chai-naasto.co.uk
**www.chai-naasto.co.uk**

# CHAI THALI

## LONDON

**Chai Thali opened its first branch in Camden in early 2017. Before you could say 'Bhel Puri' it was joined by a second eatery.**

This quirky, Bombay Café inspired restaurant is home to over 40 authentic, traditional and modern regional street food specialities. The men behind the scenes are Ajay Acharya and Sukhraj Mudhar. Both co-owners, Ajay is the restaurant's Operations Director, with a successful 25 years in the hospitality industry behind him, while Sukhraj is the Director of Finance, with experience running businesses in Mumbai and London and currently the owner of four other restaurants. Together, they've scoured the subcontinent to bring their customers the very best of Indian street food.

Rooted in tradition and bursting with aromatic spices, the menu at Chai Thali is a true reflection of authentic Indian cuisine. The food being served across the globe in India is evolving, and Chai Thali are following this movement in their restaurants.

The menu at Chai Thali features dishes from across the subcontinent; from West India they serve the Bhaaji Pao Fondue, a modern take on the Pav Bhaji. And from the South comes their ever-popular Kerala Fish Curry.

India's most-loved desserts also feature large on the menu. Try favourites such as warm grated carrots in sweet milk and the classic Kulfi in a range of flavours, then finish with a cup of Kadak Chai, widely regarded as the 'ultimate warm beverage of India'. The menu changes every quarter, and customers will often book months in advance to ensure they are among the first to try the new menu.

But it's not all about just foodies, there's the fun element as well. Chai Thali host a monthly Bollywood night as well as movie nights and art exhibitions. It's the complete night out.

**Find them at:**
Camden
19 Mandela Street, London, NW1 0DU
Tel: 020 7383 2030
Email: info@chaithali.com

Fulham
146 Wandsworth Bridge Road,London, SW6 2UH
Tel: 020 7371 8800
Email: info@chaithali.com
**www.chaithali.com**

# BHAI'S LAMB

**Serves 4**

**INGREDIENTS**

250g boneless lamb chunks
4 tablespoons oil
10g whole cumin
2 tablespoons ginger and garlic paste
4 white onions, chopped
4 tomatoes, puréed
1 tablespoon cumin powder
1 teaspoon garam masala
1 teaspoon red chilli powder
500ml water
Salt, to taste
Green chillies, to garnish
Fresh coriander leaves, to garnish

Bhai's Lamb is an authentic Punjabi Indian meat curry recipe that has been passed down by the forefathers of Chai Thali's owners. Bhai translates to brother, and this dish was created when one of the brothers of the family was hungry and decided to cook a dish himself. Once he served this to his family, they asked him what the name of the dish was, and he instantly replied 'Bhai's Lamb', claiming that it was his own original creation. This is the most popular item on Chai Thali's menu, try it for yourself and see why.

Heat the oil in a pan, add the whole cumin and fry for 1 minute.

Add the ginger and garlic paste and fry until fragrant.

Add the chopped onions and fry until they turn golden brown.

Next, add the tomato puree and cook until the colour of the tomatoes turns darker and the spices are well blended.

Add the cumin powder, coriander powder, garam masala, red chilli powder and salt and cook for a further 3 minutes.

Add the water to the pan and cover, then leave to cook for another 10 minutes over a medium heat.

Reduce to a low heat and add the lamb to the sauce, then cook for 30-90 minutes, until the lamb is cooked (cooking time will vary depending on the quality of the lamb).

Serve in a bowl topped with fried green chillies and fresh coriander leaves, with naan bread or steamed rice on the side.

# BARBECUE CHILLI BUTTER LOBSTER

**Serves 4**

**INGREDIENTS**
4 x 600-800g lobsters
6 litres water
67g salt

**SAMBHAL BASE INGREDIENTS**
500g long red chillies
1 teaspoon cumin seeds
50g ginger paste
25g garlic, crushed
150ml white wine vinegar
250ml water
2 teaspoons salt
50g sugar
75ml pure mustard oil

**CHILLI SAMBHAL BUTTER**
340g chilli sambhal base
200g butter, diced
Coriander, chopped, to taste

**Local lobster is at its best and most reasonably priced in the height of summer, and this is the only time it appears on the menu at The Chilli Pickle. The marinade is not traditional, but the ingredients and cooking methods are, and the butter blended into the fresh chilli and ginger pickle complements the sweetness of the lobster, while the rapid charring on the grill creates a delicious combination of flavours.**

### Lobster

In a large pan, bring the water to the boil and then add the salt.

To kill the live lobster immediately, place a sharp knife at the cross between the eyes and cut down to about an inch in, then wash well.

Place the lobsters in the boiling water, bring back to the boil and then turn down to simmer and cook for 7-8 minutes.

Place in iced water for 1 minute and then remove.

Remove the legs. Crack the shell with the back of a knife (being careful not to crush the meat).

Remove the claw and leg meat and set aside. Cut the main body down the middle, lengthways with a sharp knife. Remove the stomach sack and roe.

Rinse carefully under cold water so that the top shell and meat is clean of any stomach or debris.

### Sambhal Base

Wash the chillies and cut into three, then blend with the vinegar to a rough purée.

Heat a pan and add the mustard oil until smoking, then remove from heat and cool lightly.

Return the pan to the heat, add the cumin seeds and crushed garlic and cook until golden. Add the ginger paste and cook for a further minute, then add the chilli and vinegar mix, water, salt and sugar.

Simmer for approximately 15 minutes and then remove from the heat.

### Chilli Sambhal Butter

Add 340g of the chilli sambhal base to a pan.

When it starts to bubble, whisk in the cubes of fresh butter.

When the butter has been combined, add the fresh chopped coriander.

Split the sauce in half, one part to baste the lobster and one for extra sauce.

Baste the lobster tails and claws liberally as well as inside the shell and under the tail.

Cook both sides on a hot barbecue, a few minutes on each side until the meat is sizzling and lightly charred, and still tender.

Place the claws in the empty part of the shell.

# THE CHILLI PICKLE
## BRIGHTON, GUILDFORD

**India is a land rich and diverse in culture, climate and religion and as a creative chef, Alun Sperring feels he's lucky to have the opportunity to explore it.**

Alun and his wife Dawn opened The Chilli Pickle in 2010 with the aim of creating a restaurant that they'd love to eat at themselves.

White English chef-owners are few and far between in the Indian restaurant industry. Alun's point of view and culinary experience is therefore different from his Indian counterparts, but he does not feel this is a disadvantage. On the contrary, he believes it gives him more freedom to be creative.

Alun has a huge respect for Indian heritage and tradition associated with the cuisine, and his passion alongside that of his chefs communicates itself to customers through their service staff, all of whom who are given solid training on the background and provenance of the food.

At The Chilli Pickle, they've always embraced India with all its diversity as opposed to focusing on a certain region or style, but the menu does change with the seasons. The fiery and clean flavours of the South are often emphasised more in the summer, the more dairy-rich style of the North at other times. As the styles of cuisine aren't confined to just one region, Alun and Dawn have found that they're able to appeal to a wider demographic and they've now very much become a family restaurant.

The couple travel to India with their children as a family every year in search of new experiences and culinary adventure, since they are firmly of the opinion that complacency in this industry is dangerous hence the need to work hard to maintain their customers and well-earned reputation.

**Find them at:**

17 Jubilee Street, Brighton, BN1 1GE
Tel: 01273 900 383

219 High Street, Guildford, GU1 3BJ
Tel: 01483 388101
**www.thechillipickle.com**

# CHIT CHAAT CHAI

## LONDON

**Chaat…it's the staple of bustling, busy, colourful Indian streetlife. Not, as you might think, an Indian word for a good gossip, chaat is actually an umbrella term for street food.**

Chit Chaat Chai is a celebration of this, and Tania Rahman and her team pride themselves on the fact that their food celebrates the diversity of Chaat across all corners of India and beyond.

The restaurant itself has been up and running in Wandsworth since 2016, but prior to this it traded as a street stall across Hampshire and London and even ran multiple sell-out pop-ups and supper clubs. This was a pivotal part of getting Chit Chaat Chai to where it is today, as it allowed them to grow their customer base and know that making the leap from street stall to fully-fledged restaurant wouldn't be too big a risk.

Chit Chaat Chai was funded and founded by Tania herself. She was young and had little to no experience when it came to opening a restaurant. Despite the challenges she faced as a woman in this male-dominated industry, Chit Chaat Chai is now a successful business and has already won numerous awards, including Best New Business and Entrepreneur of the Year.

The presence that Chit Chaat Chai has on social media has helped them to reach more than just their local customers, and the restaurant's interior as well as the eye-catching food they serve have been described as very 'Instagrammable' by their guests. Chit Chaat Chai have even been featured on Global TV and have had customers visit them from as far afield as Dubai after having seen them on screen.

When it comes to the dishes that are served, you'll find food inspired by the regions of Maharashtra, Bengal and Goa, and everywhere in between. Tania believes that there is no longer room for toned-down dishes that are aimed at the general masses. So rest assured that your plate will be full of authentic flavours that you'd find if you'd just got off the plane in India.

**Find them at:**

356 Old York Road, Wandsworth, London, SW18 1SS

Tel: 020 8480 2364

Email: bookings@chitchaatchai.com

**www.chitchaatchai.com**

# OKRA FRIES

**INGREDIENTS**

3 tablespoons ginger and garlic paste
6 tablespoons chilli powder
300g box fresh okra, sliced through the middle
8 tablespoons corn flour
8 tablespoons gram flour

**MASALA MIX**

1 tablespoon chilli powder
1 tablespoon chaat masala
Pinch salt

**The most popular dish at Chit Chaat Chai, these crispy and crunchy okra fries have been converting even the biggest okra haters. Due to their moreish nature they often don't survive longer than a few minutes on the table. Vegan and gluten-free, these fries can cater to all so you won't have to worry about those picky eaters.**

Shake all ingredients for the masala mix together until evenly mixed and keep to one side.

Mix the ginger and garlic paste together with the chilli powder.

Coat the sliced okra in the paste and keep to one side for approximately 1-2 hours to allow the okra to marinate.

Combine the corn and gram flours in a bowl.

Coat the okra in the flour mixture.

Deep fry the okra fries until hard and crisp (approximately 3 minutes).*

Sprinkle with the masala mix.

Serve.

*If you do not have a deep fryer, add some oil to a frying pan until boiling hot and fry the okra fries, making sure to turn them so that they don't burn.

# KULFI AND GULAB JAMUN

**Makes 10**

**INGREDIENTS**

**KULFI**

1 litre whole fat milk
100g sugar
100ml double cream
50g honey
50g fresh ginger, chopped
Pinch salt

**POMEGRANATE CAVIAR**

1 litre cold vegetable oil
50g sugar
2g agar agar
10ml pomegranate molasses*
100ml water

**GULAB JAMUN**

200g sugar
3g green cardamom
500ml water
2 drops lemon juice
125g milk powder
2g baking powder
120ml water
1 tablespoon ghee
3 tablespoons milk
Vegetable oil, for frying
Few rose petals, for garnish

**Can be found in any Asian or Middle-Eastern supermarket*

A popular frozen dairy dessert often described as traditional Indian ice-cream, Kulfi does share some similarities to the dessert loved around the world. Originating from the Mughal Empire in the 16th century, this sweet treat was originally flavoured with pistachios and saffron. Chokhi Dhani serve their take on Kulfi with honey and ginger, but there are plenty of other flavour combinations that work just as well. Served with a pomegranate caviar and Gulab Jamun, this dessert is the perfect way to round off an evening, and as Kulfi takes longer to melt than ice-cream, you'll get to enjoy the dish for longer than you would your usual bowl of vanilla or chocolate.

### Kulfi

Boil the milk until it reduces to about 300ml, then add the sugar.

Add the double cream and keep on a low heat.

Mix together the honey, ginger and salt and then add to the mixture.

Pour into desired mould (eg. 2.5cm x 2.5cm) and leave to rest in the freezer overnight.

### Pomegranate Caviar

Chill the vegetable oil in the fridge.

Dissolve the remaining ingredients in a saucepan over a low heat.

Pour the mixture into a sauce bottle.

Drop by drop, add to chilled vegetable oil.

Remove drops from the oil and put in cold water and strain.

### Gulab Jamun

Boil together the sugar, green cardamom, water and lemon juice until it becomes a thin syrup, then remove from the heat and set aside.

In a large bowl, mix together the milk powder, baking powder, water, ghee and milk, then knead softly.

Separate the mixture and roll into ten equal balls.

Heat the oil in a frying pan over a medium heat (roughly 140°C) and fry the balls until golden brown.

Place the balls in the syrup and leave to absorb the flavours.

### To serve

Place a few kulfis asymmetrically on a shallow plate, adding the pomegranate caviar, then adding the gulab jamuns in line with the kulfi.

Add the rose petals to garnish.

# CHOKHI DHANI

## LONDON

**Introducing a relative newcomer among the ranks of our 50 chosen restaurants. Kriti Vaswani opened the first Chokhi Dhani in April 2018. The first outside India, that is.**

It's a long way from Rajasthan to Nine Elms Lane in South West London. But Chokhi Dhani has been cooking up the authentic taste of that region since the original restaurant was opened near Jaipur in 1990. It was run by Kriti's father Gul, who wanted the restaurant to celebrate Rajasthani culture. He did this by introducing it to local and international travellers, and the restaurant grew from just one location to a huge 22-acre, five-star star resort and event park, and now includes numerous resorts across India.

Kriti takes inspiration from what her father started back in India. If you're a bit peckish and you wander into Chokhi Dhani for a bite to eat, rest assured the restaurant's beautiful interiors and long list of entertainment will keep you there long after you thought you'd be back at home with your feet up. Chokhi Dhani's walls are adorned with bespoke artwork, and the restaurant's lounge bar celebrates traditional Rajasthani entertainment with the participation of musicians, henna artists, dancers, palmists and magicians. They even have their own on-site bazaar where you can purchase beautiful and intricate jewellery.

The Chokhi Dhani experience is about far more than merely curry. Kriti hopes customers will take away with them an understanding and appreciation for India's culture, history and way of life.

Of course, cultural matters aside, there are other things that keep customers coming back to Chokhi Dhani and that's the quality of the food. The kitchen is setting itself an ambitious target – the goal is nothing less than taking the crown as the premier Indian restaurant in South West London.

Vishnu Natarajan, Chokhi Dhani's head chef works alongside Bhagwan Singh, a globally-renowned expert on Rajasthani cuisine to create the menu that their customers know and love. With signature dishes such as their Kadak Momo Basket (crispy homemade dumplings in a matchstick potato basket served with an array of chutneys) and their Chettinad Chicken Lollipops, Chokhi Dhani know how to stand out from the hundreds of Indian restaurants in London.

**Find them at:**

2 Riverlight Quay, Nine Elms Lane<br>
London, SW11 8AW<br>
Tel: 020 3795 9000<br>
Email: info@chokhidhani.co.uk<br>
**www.chokhidhani.co.uk**

# CINNAMON BAZAAR

## LONDON

**Vivek Singh is not a man who takes his job lightly. Working tirelessly throughout the year to ensure his restaurants Cinnamon Club, Cinnamon Bazaar and Cinnamon Kitchen are running as smoothly as possible, he has brought high quality Indian cuisine to diners across London.**

Cinnamon Bazaar offers diners a variety of modern Indian dishes inspired by the marketplaces that lie on the various trading routes connecting the empires of the Old World. Their innovative dining concept mixes real Indian heritage with urban London, and this cross-cultural dining experience truly embraces the democratic spirit of the bazaar.

It's a real cultural melting pot. But to most visitors, more important is the fact that it's a good place to eat, drink, relax and celebrate. It's a place you can head to at any time of day or night, whether it's for a feast with your family or for a friendly chat over a chai.

Cinnamon Bazaar's lunch and dinner menus feature ingredients, spices and flavours that have stood the test of time. Incorporating cultural influences from all over the world, their Chicken Haleem connects India with Iran, their Millet, Date, Tamarind and Pomegranate Salad pays homage to the markets of the Middle East and their Lahore Chicken Kadhai connects Old Delhi to new Lahore, a popular trading route.

Dating as far back as the 1600s, bazaar traders would often work long days and indulge in the savoury snack, chaat. To this day, chaat continues to be one of India's most popular street foods, and Cinnamon Bazaar are proud to have their own unique range of chaats.

They've also got the perfect range of drinks to complement each dish, and their cocktail menu designed by Ryan Chetiyawardan with its scents, flavours and colours, will only add to the journey you're taking to another world. All aboard the magic carpet!

**Find them at:**
28 Maiden Lane, Covent Garden, London, WC2E 7JS
Tel: 0207 395 1400
Email: info@cinnamon-bazaar.com
**cinnamon-bazaar.com**

# LAMB GALOUTI KEBAB

**Serves 4**

**INGREDIENTS**

500g lean lamb leg meat, minced
3 teaspoons ginger and garlic paste
1 ½ tablespoons red chilli powder
3 tablespoons ghee, melted
1 pinch saffron, soaked in 2 tablespoons water
1 teaspoon fresh pineapple juice or 1 teaspoon green papaya, grated
1 ½ teaspoons salt
4 tablespoons dried onions, fried
2 tablespoons fried cashew nut paste

**SPICE MIX**

½ teaspoon cumin, roasted and cooled
4 green cardamoms
1 blade mace
Seeds of 1 black cardamom
1 teaspoon black peppercorns
1/8 nutmeg
8 cloves, seeded

**A favourite across all of the Cinnamon restaurants, the Galouti kebab is a gift from Lucknow in central India; a tender kebab with an explosion of flavours that should melt in your mouth, with some describing them as an Indian version of pate. While the original kebabs used beef, today lamb is a more popular choice.**

Keep aside six cloves and mix together the remainder of the spices for the spice mix and grind to a fine powder in a mortar and pestle.

Heat 2 tablespoons of ghee in a small pan and add the remaining cloves, leave them to pop for around 30 seconds to release their flavours, remove from the heat and let cool.

Add the lamb to a mixing bowl, add the spice mix and the remainder of the ingredients (except the remaining ghee) and mix well.

Add the clove-infused ghee into the mince and chill for 10 minutes.

Take the chilled mince and add the remaining tablespoon of ghee, mix thoroughly and refrigerate again to chill.

Shape the meat into patties of about 40 to 50g each and about 4cm in diameter.

Heat some extra ghee in a heavy-based frying pan and shallow fry the patties over a low heat for about 1-2 minutes on each side until they are well cooked.

Remove from the pan and place them on kitchen paper to remove any excess fat.

Serve hot.

# TANDOORI GROUSE WITH AUBERGINE CRUSH

**Serves 4**

**INGREDIENTS**

4 whole grouse*

**FIRST MARINADE**

1 teaspoon ginger paste
1 teaspoon garlic paste
½ teaspoon salt
1 teaspoon lemon juice

**SECOND MARINADE**

1 tablespoon vegetable oil
50g whole cashew nut paste*
½ teaspoon cumin seeds, roasted and powdered
6 cloves, roasted and powdered

**FOR LEG MINCE**

1 ½ tablespoons ghee or butter
1 teaspoon cumin seeds
1 teaspoon black onion seeds
1 teaspoon fennel seeds
1 teaspoon mustard seeds
2 cloves garlic, chopped
½ medium-sized onion, chopped
½ teaspoon chilli powder
¼ teaspoon salt
1 tomato, deseeded and diced
15g coriander leaves, chopped

**AUBERGINE CRUSH**

2 large aubergines
2 tablespoons oil
1 teaspoon cumin
3 cloves garlic, chopped
1 large onion, finely chopped
1 teaspoon red chilli powder
1 teaspoon roasted ground cumin
2 tomatoes, chopped
1 inch ginger, finely chopped
2 green chillies, chopped
1 ¼ teaspoon ground garam masala
4g fresh coriander, chopped

**While there are no grouse in India, Cinnamon Club is very popular for its game dishes. This is a simple dish to cook and has a strong yet stunning flavour. You can ask your butcher to prepare your grouse for you, and pop down to your local supermarket for some paratha or wraps to serve alongside the dish.**

### For the grouse breasts

Clean and trim the grouse breasts, then marinate in the first marinade and leave for 30 minutes.

Add oil, then rub in the cashew paste and sprinkle the powdered cumin and cloves over the grouse, then mix well and leave for another 30 minutes.

To cook the breasts, either use a tandoori oven or sear the breasts in a pan and finish off in a moderately hot oven (180-200°C) for 6-8 minutes.

### For the grouse mince

Heat the ghee in a pan, then add the cumin seeds, black onion seeds, fennel seeds and mustard seeds and once it starts to crackle, add the chopped garlic.

When the garlic starts to brown, add the onions until golden brown and then add the grouse mince and the chilli powder and cook until almost dry.

Add the salt and diced tomatoes and then add the coriander leaves shortly before removing from the heat.

### For the aubergine crush

Preheat the oven to 180-200°C.

Rub a little oil on the aubergine and roast in the oven for 20 minutes, turning halfway through.

When the skin starts to wrinkle and soften, allow the aubergine to cool, peel the skin and mash.

Heat oil in a pan, add the cumin seeds and when they begin to crackle, add the garlic and sauté.

When the garlic starts to brown, add the onions and sauté until brown.

Add the chilli and cumin powders and cook for 30 seconds, then add tomatoes and cook until soft.

Add the ginger and green chillies, then mix in the mashed aubergine and stir well for 2 minutes.

Add salt and fresh coriander and sprinkle with garam masala, then after 30 seconds remove from the heat.

# THE CINNAMON CLUB
## LONDON

**There can be few Indian restaurants in the country in a grander setting than the Cinnamon Club. The imposing historic Grade II listed former Westminster Library has been home to the restaurant since it opened in 2001.**

But for owner and executive chef Vivek Singh, the magnificent surroundings are only part of the story. His stated aim is to be challenging and rewriting the rule book on Indian cuisine.

In this Vivek is inspired by the experiences he had as a child brought up in Asansol, India. As Asansol had a strong Anglo influence, he grew up celebrating both Christian and Hindu festivals, enabling him to learn about many different cuisines. Today, Vivek still combines these two cultures, mixing Indian spices and flavours with Western techniques and ingredients.

The menu at The Cinnamon Club has evolved over the years, as Vivek and his team refuse to believe that Indian cuisine should stay stuck in the past, instead believing that 'innovation today forms the basis of tradition tomorrow'. The Cinnamon Club's menu features dishes from across India rather than focusing on just one region, and their unique take on game classics and delicately spiced fish are favourites of their diners.

The Cinnamon Club take pride in their involvement with numerous charities, with the team taking a particular interest in helping young people from deprived communities. Vivek is a member of the Asian Restaurant Skills Board which supports the Mastara Chef initiative – their goal is to raise awareness and promote career opportunities in Asian and Oriental cuisine by offering apprenticeships in some of London's finest Indian restaurants. The Cinnamon Club also host their own 'day in the life' experiences with the Mosaic charity, where young students spend a day in the kitchen with Vivek to get an understanding of what it's like to work in a busy restaurant.

Never a dull moment in Vivek's life, alongside running The Cinnamon Club he also runs Cinnamon Bazaar and Cinnamon Kitchen branches in the City of London, Oxford and Battersea.

**Find them at:**

The Old Westminster Library,
30-32 Great Smith Street, London, SW1P 3BU
Tel: 020 7222 255
**www.thecinnamoncollection.com**

# CINNAMON CULTURE

## BROMLEY

**There's no substitute for the personal touch. You know, the sort of place where they can tell at a glance that you've had THAT kind of a week, and sympathetically administer a suitable remedy in the shape of an ice-cold Kingfisher. It's the sort of place where they know the customers by name and understand their individual preferences. A bit like home, really.**

This family-run restaurant, headed up by a husband and wife duo, seeks to provide their customers with the kind of food that they would prepare for themselves at home. Their ever-changing a la carte menu contains dishes from all over India and offers up seasonal regional specials such as North Indian game and coastal specialities. Their menu also frequently offers themed dishes, such as some that are considered tandoori delicacies or food that would be found on menus from the royal courts of India.

Cinnamon Culture is not chasing awards or recognition from anyone other than those who come through their doors and share their love for traditional Indian cuisine. Yet

Cinnamon Culture has grown to become more popular with those living some distance from its Bromley base.

Their choice of recipe for this book illustrates perfectly their philosophy on food. This dish was introduced to their menu in 2013 and it quickly caught the eye of the late Peter Grove, the founder of National Curry Week, who declared it the Best Traditional Signature Dish of the Year.

**Find them at:**
Plaistow Lane, Bromley, BR1 3PA
Tel: 0208 289 0322
Email: info@cinnamonculture.com
**www.cinnamonculture.com**

# WILD MADAGASCAN PRAWNS WITH SHRIMP KEDGEREE & ALLEPPEY SAUCE

## (SERVE WITH MIXED GREEN LEAF AND JULIENNE PEPPER SALAD)

**Serves 2**

**INGREDIENTS**

**PRAWN MARINADE**

2 wild Madagascan prawns, frozen
1 tablespoon ginger, grated
1 tablespoon garlic, grated
1 teaspoon Kashmiri chilli powder*
1 teaspoon turmeric powder
1 tablespoon lemon juice
1 tablespoon oil
Salt, to taste

**SHRIMP KEDGEREE**

150g shrimps
2-3 tablespoons oil
2 medium onions, chopped
2 fresh tomatoes, chopped
1 tablespoon cumin seeds
10g garlic, chopped
10 ginger, chopped
1 teaspoon chilli powder (deggi merch*)
1 teaspoon turmeric powder
185g basmati rice, rinsed until the water runs clear
185g moong daal, rinsed until the water runs clear
700ml water
1 tablespoon lemon juice
Salt, to taste

**ALLEPPEY SAUCE**

1 tablespoon sunflower oil
1 teaspoon garlic, finely chopped
1 small onion, finely chopped
100ml plum tomatoes or 2 good quality large tomatoes, chopped
1 teaspoon turmeric powder
1 teaspoon chilli powder
1 teaspoon lemon juice
100ml coconut milk
Pinch of sugar
Salt, to taste

** Available from your local Asian supermarket or specialist food shop*

**Most of us know of the Anglo-Indian classic, Kedgeree with Fish and Eggs, as adapted by the Victorians from the popular Indian dish Khichri. With the exception of the addition of the shrimps, Cinnamon Culture have kept as true to the original recipe as possible. This dish was introduced to their menu in 2013 and it quickly caught the eye of the late Peter Grove, the founder of the National Curry Week, who awarded it the title of the Best Traditional Signature Dish of the Year.**

### Prawns

Preheat oven to 200°C on grill setting.

Wash the prawns and remove the legs. Devein and cut across from head to tail, then wash again and pat dry.

Combine all the marinade ingredients in a small bowl and apply to the prawns. Leave in the fridge for 15-30 minutes to marinate.

Once marinated, grill for 8 minutes.

### Alleppey Sauce

Heat the oil in a pan, add the chopped garlic and gently sauté until light brown.

Add the chopped onion and cook on a low heat for 2-3 minutes until soft.

Add all remaining ingredients (except coconut milk), combine well and cook for further 2 minutes.

Add the coconut milk, stir in and keep on a low heat until the mixture becomes sauce-like in texture.

### Shrimp Kedgeree

Heat the oil in a saucepan over a medium heat, add the chopped garlic and cumin seeds, sauté until the seeds crackle.

Add the chopped onions and sauté until golden brown.

Add the chopped ginger and sauté for additional minute until fragrant.

Stir in the turmeric, chilli and tomatoes and cook for another minute.

Toss in the prawns and heat through for 1-2 minutes, stirring gently from time to time.

Add the washed rice and daal, lemon juice and water, stir carefully and add salt to taste.

Bring to boil and cover, then reduce the heat and simmer for approximately 15-20 minutes.

Serve with a salad of mixed green leaves and julienne peppers to add a touch of colour, and a wedge of lime.

# AUBERGINE BHAJIS

**Serves 4**

**INGREDIENTS**

200ml vegetable oil
100g rice flour
100g gram (chickpea) flour
25g ginger, minced
25g garlic, minced
30g chilli powder
20g aiwain (carom) seeds
20g turmeric powder
50ml fresh lemon juice
Salt, to taste
2 large aubergines (approx. 400g), sliced into 5mm rounds

**Some of India's finest food can be found at street-side stalls (or dhabbas) manned by skilled men or women, often serving just a single dish – like these aubergine bhajis. These bhajis are equally as popular in the Curry Leaf Café restaurants as well as in West Bengal, where head chef Gouranga Bera grew up. Great on their own and when paired with a mango or tamarind chutney for dipping, and some say even better when paired with a cold pint of beer!**

Heat the oil in a deep-sided saucepan to 180°C.

Place all ingredients except the aubergines into a large bowl.

Add 200ml of water to the bowl, pouring slowly while mixing with a whisk into a thick, smooth batter.

Dip the aubergine slices in the batter and carefully lower into the hot oil.

Fry the aubergines until they turn a dark brown (approximately 4-5 minutes), making sure not to add too many to the pan at once as the slices need space around them to cook properly.

Remove the cooked slices with a slotted spoon and place on a paper towel to dry.

Serve immediately, with or without chutney.

# CURRY LEAF CAFÉ
## BRIGHTON

**Curry Leaf Café is the brainchild of former food journalist Euan Sey, and Chef Kanthi Thamma, who met in 2013 after becoming flatmates. They soon discovered they had something in common, and that was a love of good food. As a child, Euan would be taken out for a curry as his birthday treat each year. Kanthi on the other hand grew up in India. He had long dreamed of opening up a small lunch-only café in the UK. Armed with recipes from his childhood and his experience of working in kitchens through all of his adult life, and Euan's knowledge of branding, design and an understanding of how to run the business side of things, they were the perfect pair.**

Since the opening of their first restaurant, the Brighton Lanes Café in April 2014, the pair went on to open a second location in the Kemptown quarter of Brighton, featuring a unique open kitchen and dining space serving tapas-style Indian dishes. In 2016 the two became the first to open an Indian street food kiosk inside a UK train station. Their locations are not what would be expected from an Indian restaurant, and this is because Curry Leaf Café is just that - a café – which has become popular with locals looking to avoid the masses of tourists visiting Brighton in the summer. Visitors are greeted by a relaxed atmosphere; bricks, bright colours and graffiti adorn the walls here, with large windows flooding the interior with light and music playing in the background. While the aesthetics of their locations certainly grab the attention, it's their short but diverse menu that sets them apart and keeps people returning.

In 2017 Kanthi left the brand to pursue personal projects and his close friend Gouranga Bera took over the kitchen. Influenced highly by the rich histories and flavours of Kerala and Hyderabad, Gouranga's menu changes with the seasons, encouraging their customers to come back and try something new. Whatever the time of year, though, South Indian street food is always their speciality. Euan and his team hope to go on to look outside of Brighton for a third restaurant location.

**Find them at:**

Brighton Lanes Café
60 Ship Street, Brighton, East Sussex, BN1 1AE
Tel: 01273 207070
Email: brighton@curryleafcafe.com

Kemptown Kitchen
40-42 Upper St James' Street, Brighton, East Sussex, BN2 1JN
Tel: 01273 526910
Email: kemptown@curryleafcafe.com

Brighton Station Kiosk
Main Concourse, Queens Road, Brighton, East Sussex, BN1 3XP
Email: kiosk@curryleafcafe.com

**www.curryleafcafe.com**

# DAKHIN
## GLASGOW

**Indian cuisine has always held a special place in the heart of Scotland, but by the early 2000s the food being served in its Indian restaurants had started to look and taste all too similar.**

Glasgow restaurateur Navdeep Basi decided that it was the perfect time for some innovative disruption and in August 2004, Dakhin was born. The first South Indian restaurant to open in Scotland, Dakhin serves traditional, unique and often unheard of dishes that challenge their customers' notions of what Indian cuisine really is.

Dakhin is the first and only Indian restaurant in the UK to offer a 100 per cent gluten-free menu – including their breads and desserts. The dishes served here are also mostly dairy-free and plenty of veggie and vegan-friendly option are available in plenty. Designed by a team of chefs who all come from different parts of southern India, the menu has always been a group effort, with each member of the team bringing their own traditions and perspectives to the menu. Influenced by the cuisine of Andhra Pradesh, Karnataka, Tamil Nadu and Kerala, to name but a few, the menu has evolved over the years but much of the team and the menu's concepts have remained unchanged.

Dakhin's relaxed yet stylish interior is most inviting, and the view of the kitchen from across the restaurant means that there's no lack of entertainment as the expert chefs effortlessly prepare in a matter of minutes dishes and breads that would take hours upon hours to create at home. A few quick hand movements, a puff of flame and it's ready to serve. Blink and you'll miss it.

**Find them at:**

89 Candleriggs, Merchant City, Glasgow, G1 1NP

Tel: 0141 553 2585

Email: info@dakhin.com

**www.dakhin.com**

# THENAGAI MITHAI

**Makes 15**

**INGREDIENTS**

750ml whole milk
1kg powdered milk
500ml coconut milk
50g desiccated coconut
150g powdered sugar
5g cardamom powder

A treasured homemade recipe from the southern region of India, this coconut fudge is definitely for those with a sweet tooth. Perfectly dense, creamy and rich, this dish is bursting with real coconut flavour with a hint of cardamom. Dakhin recommend adding 50g of powdered cashew nuts along with the cardamom powder for an extra kick of flavour. This recipe makes 15 servings so is great for dishing out at any family or kids party, and can be kept refrigerated for a week in case you fancy sneaking to the fridge for a midnight snack.

Line a 12x12 pan with aluminium foil and spray the foil with non-stick cooking spray.

In a large saucepan, heat the milk until it starts to boil.

Reduce the heat and add the milk powder and coconut milk.

Stir well until the mixture starts to thicken (usually about 7-10 minutes).

Add the desiccated coconut, powdered sugar and cardamom powder to the mixture and continue stirring on a low heat.

Keep stirring for a further 7-10 minutes until it starts to reach a thick and sticky consistency.

Scrape the mixture into the prepared pan and smooth into an even layer.

Leave to cool at room temperature for approximately 30 minutes.

Refrigerate for a few hours until set.

Once set, cut into even squares and serve cold with an extra sprinkle of desiccated coconut.

# KASUNDI MOOLI LAMB CHOPS

## SERVED WITH BASMATI RICE

**Serves 2**

**INGREDIENTS**

1kg French trimmed, 8 bone rack of lamb, cut into 3-4cm ribs

**FIRST MARINADE**

1 x 4cm piece bruised ginger, whole and unpeeled
45g ginger and garlic paste
10g dried fenugreek leaves, ground
7.5g salt
40g Kashmiri chilli powder
25ml lemon juice
45ml mustard oil

**SECOND MARINADE**

300g hung Greek yoghurt
2 green chillies, finely chopped
15g ginger and garlic paste
7.5g turmeric
5g dried fenugreek leaves, ground
10g Kashmiri chilli powder
15g garam masala

**The most popular dish at Dastaan, their lamb chops cooked in their signature marinade are constantly attracting positive feedback to the kitchen. Dastaan has a policy of listening, and reacting to, their diners' comments.**
**For best results, pop down to your local butcher and getting them to trim and prepare your lamb chops for you. Dastaan also recommend marinating the meat for 2-3 days.**

Tenderise the lamb chops with a meat mallet.

Place the lamb chops in a bowl and add all of the ingredients for the first marinade.

Mix the marinade well into the lamb chops, then leave to refrigerate for at least 12-36 hours.

Once the lamb chops have had plenty of time to soak in the first marinade, add Leave to marinate in the fridge for up to another 12 hours.

Preheat the oven to 220°C.

Thread the lamb onto skewers, passing them two or three times through each piece to secure well.

Place the skewers in the oven for 5 minutes at 220°C, then reduce the temperature to 180°C and cook for a further 7 minutes.

Remove the lamb shanks from the oven and sprinkle with a little chaat masala before serving.

# DASTAAN
## EPSOM

**Nand Kishor and Sanjay Gour opened Dastaan two years ago, both with a wealth of culinary experience behind them and driven by a passion for Indian cuisine that never gave their restaurant any option but to succeed. Dastaan has already received numerous accolades, being presented with a Michelin Bib Gourmand and an AA rosette.**

Both Nand and Sanjay have previously occupied the role of Head Chef at Gymkhana, one of the most talked about Michelin-starred Indian restaurants in London and now their ambition is for Dastaan to become Epsom's equivalent. At Dastaan it's all about bringing authentic Indian cuisine to a new age, and they've chosen not to focus on just one region but rather to embrace the freedom that comes with allowing themselves to explore the subcontinent in all its glory.

Dastaan's signature dishes include their Red Pepper Tiger Prawns, Tandoori Lamb Chops and the highly popular Duck and Guinea Fowl Sheek Kebabs, all of which are flavourful and beautifully presented examples of how they're achieving their aim of bringing the flair of Mayfair calibre restaurants to their own local Surrey curry house. Their menu also boasts the indulgent Tellicherry Dorset Crab and Pork Vindaloo, as well as vegetarian options such as Paneer Makhani and Aubergine Masala.

There's no sign of any slowing down at Dastaan. In fact Nand and Sanjay already have in place a long list of projects.

Plans are afoot for opening further branches as well as forging partnerships with other restaurants across the country, and they're passionate about helping talented chefs get started in the Indian food industry.

Find them at:
447 Kingston Road, Epsom, KT19 0DB
Tel: 020 8786 8999
Email: info@dastaan.co.uk (non booking enquiries)
dastaan.booking@gmail.com (bookings only)
**www.dastaan.co.uk**

# THE DHABBA
## GLASGOW

In 2002, The Dhabba opened in one of Glasgow's oldest quarters, paying homage to the many namesakes from the old country. In case you're wondering, back in North India, a dhabba is a family-run, roadside diners that captivate hungry travellers with their own menu of closely-guarded recipes that were often passed on from father to son and mother to daughter.

A transport caff it certainly is not. Over time the food from the dhabbas managed to spread from the highways into the cities, with hotels starting to adapt their menus to integrate the concept of the dhabba into their own restaurants.

Handpicked chefs from across Northern India have come together at The Dhabba and created a unique menu offering a wide range of dishes, constantly innovating and refining their original concept to encourage Glaswegians to try true authentic North Indian cuisine. The Dhabba have played host to patrons from all over the UK and around the world, with famous Hollywood and Bollywood faces even popping up on occasion.

While they want to stay true to their roots, the chefs at The Dhabba are well aware of what their customers are starting to expect when they choose to dine out. With people generally preferring to opt for healthier, lighter food, the owners have reinvented their menu to keep up with not only what the customers are demanding, but to continue to reflect the changes that are happening back in India. When celebrating their 15th anniversary they completely updated their menu to ensure that they wouldn't render themselves forgettable, and even chose to include street food for the first time. The Dhabba have made themselves at home in Glasgow, and they want to ensure that home is what it remains in the years to come.

**Find them at:**

44 Candleriggs, Merchant City,
Glasgow, G1 1LD
Tel: 0141 553 1249
Email: 0141 553 1249
**www.thedhabba.com**

# MURG-E-CHANGEZI

## SERVE WITH RICE OR INDIAN BREADS

**Serves 4**

**INGREDIENTS**

**FOR THE CHICKEN**

- 4 chicken supreme (chicken breast with the first joint of the wing still attached)
- 10g ginger and garlic paste
- 5ml lemon juice
- 5g red chilli powder
- 10g tandoori masala powder
- 5g coriander powder
- 5g dried fenugreek leaves
- 20g yoghurt
- 10g vegetable oil
- 7g salt

**FOR THE SAUCE**

- 600ml oil
- 5g cumin seeds
- 1 Spanish onion, finely chopped
- 15g ginger and garlic paste
- 5g turmeric powder
- 10g red chilli powder
- 10g coriander powder
- 10g cumin powder
- 120g tomato, finely chopped
- 25g yoghurt
- 15g khus khus (poppy seeds)
- 15g charmagaz (mixed melon seeds)
- 10g salt
- 5g cardamom powder
- 5g garam masala
- 30ml single cream
- 30g unsalted butter
- 10g coriander leaves
- 470ml water

**The Murg-E-Changezi, famous in the streets of Old Delhi, is named after none other than the Mongolian ruler and invader Genghis Khan, or Changez Khan as he is known in India. Legend has it that he was extremely particular about his food and the spices used in it. One of his chefs experimented with a range of spices, cream and yoghurt to create the Murg-E-Changezi – a chicken dish that turned out to be Khan's favourite. Guests at The Dhabba are advised that it takes around thirty minutes for this dish to reach their table - and it's well worth the wait!**

Mix together all of the ingredients for the chicken in a bowl.

Set aside for 4-6 hours to allow the chicken to marinate.

Once the chicken has had time to marinate, preheat the oven to 160°C

Heat the oil in a saucepan over a medium heat.

Add the cumin seeds until they begin to crackle.

Add the chopped onions and cook until they turn golden brown.

Add the ginger and garlic paste, turmeric, red chilli, coriander and cumin powders and mix well.

Add the tomatoes and yoghurt and cook for 2-3 minutes until the mixture becomes smooth.

Add the water, charmagaz, khus khus and salt.

Cook for about 10 minutes on a low heat until it starts to boil.

Using a hand blender, blend the mixture until smooth.

Add the cardamom powder, garam masala, butter and half of the cream.

Bake the chicken on a skewer for 7-8 minutes so the inside stays soft and juicy while the outside is browned.

Trim the browned parts of the chicken to shreds and set aside.

Make deep cuts into the chicken breast.

Mix the shredded chicken trimmings into the cooked sauce.

Pour generously over the chicken.

Garnish with coriander and the rest of the cream.

Serve with rice or Indian bread.

# GAR-LICK WINGS WITH DESINNAISE

**Makes 15**

**INGREDIENTS**

15 whole chicken wings, skin on

**MARINADE**

4 tablespoons extra virgin olive oil
2 tablespoons ginger and garlic paste
2 tablespoons white distilled vinegar
1 tablespoon natural yoghurt
1 teaspoon tomato puree
1 teaspoon smoked sea salt
2 teaspoons fenugreek leaves, crushed
1 teaspoon coarse black pepper
1 teaspoon coriander seeds
½ teaspoon red chilli powder
½ teaspoon garam masala
½ teaspoon garlic and coriander seasoning

**DESINNAISE**

5 tablespoons mayonnaise
1 ½ tablespoons coriander, finely chopped
1 teaspoon red chilli powder
½ teaspoon roasted cumin seeds
Pinch chaat masala

**GARNISH**

Salad leaves
Coriander, chopped

**Many of Dipna's family and friends often ask her to make her special chicken wings with her mouth-watering masala mayonnaise she now calls desinnaise. At first reluctant to give out her secret recipe, Dipna has now shared the dish on her television series, Dip in Kitchen, and they've been such a hit that she often adds them to the specials menu at her restaurants.**

Pre-heat the oven to 160°C.

Mix together all the ingredients for the marinade in a food blender.

Coat the chicken wings in the marinade and leave to marinate for at least 30 minutes (ideally overnight if you've got the time).

While the chicken is marinating, make the desinnaise by mixing together all of the ingredients, then leave to refrigerate.

Once the chicken has marinated for long enough, place the wings on an oven tray and roast in the oven for 20-25 minutes, checking them every 5 minutes or so and giving them a turn or two.

Serve with the desinnaise and enjoy.

# DIP IN BRILLIANT

## LONDON

**Dip in Brilliant is a trendy Punjabi cafe/restaurant in Fulham (located next to Chelsea Football Club) led by celebrity chef Dipna Anand of Southall's original Brilliant Restaurant.**

Dipna's passion and drive to take Punjabi food to a completely new level was a dream realised with the opening of her Dip in Brilliant dream.

Her father Gulu and Uncle Kewal opened the first Brilliant Restaurant in London in 1975 and her brother Shanker continues in flying the flag alongside his father. The restaurant had its roots in the place founded by Bishen Dass Anand, who opened the first Brilliant restaurant, nightclub and hotel back in Kenya in the 1950s. Dipna continues to re-create her grandfather's recipes which date back 65 years.

In the hands of son Gulu, The Brilliant became an astonishing success story, with it fame spreading far beyond its base in Southall. Aided by the success of a bestselling book, it provided the platform to propel Dipna into the ranks of TV chefs.

Dip in Brilliant is an eatery with a retro and trendy dining concept. Dipna says is all about 'keeping things real'. She believes Dip in Brilliant is a place where punters can dip in and out of within 30 minutes if they're under time pressure or alternatively somewhere they can sit and enjoy a long lunch. Dip in Brilliant is about serving hearty Punjabi food in a casual setting. Keeping the flavours pure, the spices balanced and dishes as authentic as possible and then presenting the food in a chic fashion yet keeping somewhat of a traditional feel is the experience created when you dip in.

At Dip in Brilliant you eat from a thali (the Indian name for a metal round platter). This in Dipna's opinion creates an even more relaxing food culture and also encourages the use of hands to eat making the meal even more delicious. A Punjabi meal is about sharing and creating that atmosphere of togetherness and at Dip in Brilliant our guests become part of our family. Brilliant by name, brilliant by nature, they look forward to welcoming you.

**Find them at:**
448-450 Fulham Road, Fulham, London, SW6 1DL
Tel: 020 3771 9443
Email: info@dipinbrilliant.com
**www.dipinbrilliant.com**

# DUCHESS OF DELHI

## CARDIFF

**As the name suggests, this is an aristocrat among Indian restaurants.**

It sits proudly in a home which is certainly fit for a Duchess, in the shape of a Grade II listed building overlooking the Millennium Centre in Cardiff.

It has a colourful past. Among other things, It was formerly the residence of a Ship's Captain who plied the world's trading routes. Then, rather less romantically, the landlubbers at the Glamorgan Coal Company moved in there in 1893. It has witnessed the area grow from a coal exportation site to the area now known as Tiger Bay, and tells an entirely different story.

It's difficult not to admire the beauty of the restaurant. Duchess of Delhi used designers and artists from around the world to create their authentic Indian restaurant. Their classic interior is reflective of the luxuriously rich colours found in India, its vibrant and artistic setting inspired by the rich heritage of the Rajas and Moguls of the subcontinent.

The Mughal period in South Asia provides the restaurant's main inspiration. Mughal feasts were extravagant affairs where plentiful amounts of fruit, nuts and creamy dishes were served, often garnished with gold and silver leaf. Some of the dishes were hot, using extra chilli, while others would use valuable spices such as saffron. Duchess of Delhi embraces the traditional and lavish Mughal period while adding their own splash of modernity.

The menu consists of dishes inspired by the traditional cuisines of Nepal, Thailand, Malaysia, Singapore, Burma, Bangladesh and Sri-Lanka, each one beautifully constructed to authentically represent the elegance of the Mughal period.

Even the neighbours are foodies. The building is also home to Chaat! Magazine, dedicated to spicy food and travel, celebrating the Asian food industry twice each month and including recipes from big names such as The Hairy Bikers, Incredible Spice Men and James Martin.

**Find them at:**
6 Bute Crescent, Cardiff Bay, CF10 5AN
Tel: 029 211 53574
Email: info@duchessofdelhi.com
**www.duchessofdelhi.com**

# CHICKEN CHETTINADU

## SERVED WITH BASMATI RICE

**INGREDIENTS**

1kg chicken
1 tablespoon mustard seeds
1 teaspoon coriander seeds
1 teaspoon cumin seeds
1 teaspoon fennel seeds
3 dry red chillies
1 teaspoon crushed black pepper
1 teaspoon garam masala
1 cinnamon stick
1 star anise
2 cardamom pods
3 cloves garlic
30g grated coconut
Splash coconut milk
2 teaspoons ginger paste
2 teaspoons garlic paste
2-3 tablespoons vegetable/sunflower/canola oil
10 curry leaves
2 large onions, finely chopped
2 tomatoes, finely chopped
2 teaspoons lime juice
Salt, to taste
Coriander leaves, chopped to garnish

**One of the most popular dishes at Duchess of Delhi, the Chicken Chettinadu has a very distinct flavour, and its mustard seeds and curry leaves give it just the right amount of heat. While the spices do compliment the chicken perfectly, if you're not a meat-eater you can turn this into a vegetarian dish by simply replacing the chicken with a range of vegetables of your choice for an equally flavourful dish.**

Heat a saucepan over a medium heat, then gently roast the coriander, cumin, mustard, fennel seeds, dry red chillies, cinnamon, cardamom, cloves and coconut for 3-4 minutes.

Allow to cool, then grind the mixture until a coarse texture.

Once the mixture is cooled, mix in the ginger and garlic pastes and set aside.

In a deep pan, heat some oil, then add the curry leaves and onions and fry until light brown.

Add the black pepper, star anise and the paste you created earlier and fry for another 2-3 minutes.

Add the tomatoes and stir all ingredients together (if you want an added kick, now would be the time to add a little chilli powder).

Cut the chicken into equal chunks, then add to the sauce, cover and then simmer until the chicken is tender.

Once the chicken is cooked through, add the lime juice, mix well and turn off the heat.

Garnish with a few mustard seeds, sprinkle the garam masala, coriander leaves and serve alongside a side of basmati rice.

# SOFT SHELL CRAB AND KING PRAWN CURRY

**Serves 4**

**INGREDIENTS**

200ml coconut cream
20g tomatoes
8g coriander
12g green chillies
12g mustard
20g coriander powder
80ml Greek yoghurt
20g onion
4 soft shell crabs
80g pakora mix
360g king prawns

This dish has been adapted by Flora Indica from the more traditional curries that are served in the Eastern towns and cities of India. Instead of using fish for this recipe, the chefs at Flora Indica have preferred soft shell crab and prawns. A popular dish on their menu, this tends to win over their diners as they fall for the coconut milk and mustard flavoured sauce (one that they also use for their best-selling Monkfish Curry).

Combine the coconut cream, tomatoes, coriander, green chillies, mustard, coriander powder, Greek yoghurt and onions in a saucepan and heat through.

Coat the soft shell crab with light pakora mix and fry until crisp.

Lightly fry the king prawns.

Pour the sauce into a bowl and place the crab and the prawns on top and serve.

# FLORA INDICA

## LONDON

**Attention all you serious gardeners out there... where would you find Flora Indica?**

The Chelsea Flower Show perhaps? After all it's the kind of event that attracts aficionados who can reel off the Latin names of plants in their sleep. And the more informed among them might even add that it appears in an 1855 book of the same name, which catalogues thousands of exotic Indian plants that were previously unknown in Britain.

Just a little further down the road from the show, the influence of this milestone book is still being celebrated, in the shape of an intriguing Indian restaurant.

The botanists have got their priorities right when it comes to paying homage to the book. Many of the plants and spices it 'discovered' are put to good use in the restaurant's extensive selection of botanical gins.

Although it's a relative newcomer on the restaurant scene, Flora Indica is making a mark with its modern menu, part of a celebration of Indian culture, flavours and hospitality

The restaurant's décor also gives a nod to those who brought over the flavours and spices we know and love today, with antique distillery piping adorning the walls and Harris Tweed covering the luxurious dining chairs. Spread over two floors, Flora Indica has plenty of space for events, allowing customers to take advantage of both their main restaurant space and their two semi-private dining rooms.

The dishes served come from regions across India, making use of fresh ingredients available to them such as artichoke, samphire, octopus, soft shell crab and King Edward potatoes. The menu features small plates, and everything ordered will be beautifully presented in a modern style.

Aware that people are starting to see the difference between authentic Indian cuisine and so-called 'British Indian' food, the people behind Flora Indica are confident that customers will continue to flock to them for a taste of their own take on traditional Indian dishes.

**Find them at:**

242 Old Brompton Road, London, SW5 0DE

Tel: 020 7370 4450

Email: reservations@flora-indica.com

**www.flora-indica.com**

# GANAPATI

## LONDON

**No-one ever forgets their first trip to India. It has a way of captivating visitors like few other places can. So it's not surprising that many visitors are lured back again.**

So it was with Claire Fisher. Her experiences there were the beginning of a lifelong love-affair with the sub-continent and, as it turned out, her travels proved to be life-changing.

Claire brought back a passion for Indian cookery and an idea. It was an idea that turned into reality in the shape of Ganapati, which opened for business in Peckham, South London in December 2004.

Its name comes from one of the South Indian words for the elephant-headed God Ganesh, the well-loved remover of obstacles (and lover of sweets). Focusing on the then less well-known cuisine of southern regions of India, and in particular Kerala and Tamil Nadu, Ganapati was a restaurant with a difference.

It still is today. More than a decade later, Claire and her team of chefs are still involved in the development of the menu. Every couple of months it is changed, meaning that there's always an opportunity to feature the new recipes that she and the team have researched.

The passion that the team at Ganapati have for home-style Indian cuisine really shows in the way that they prepare each dish. Everything is made from scratch here, right down to the yoghurts and pickles.

In 2014 they opened their own home delivery shop, the Ganapati Takeaway Kitchen, not too far from the restaurant. With a menu that differs slightly, yet remains true to Ganapati's original concept, they are now able to reach more customers.

Claire believes that although the overall standard of Indian cuisine in the UK is improving, the regional areas such as Madya Pradesh and Odisha are being underrepresented, and she'd like to see more restaurants presenting more regional dishes. Claire is also passionate about the fact that we need to train young UK chefs in Indian and other specialist cuisines, as immigration rules are making it difficult to bring specialist chefs to the UK.

**Find them at:**

38 Holly Grove, London, SE15 5DF

Tel: 020 7277 2928

Email: info@ganapatirestaurant.com

**www.ganapatirestaurant.com**

## GANAPATI

**Serves 1**

**INGREDIENTS**

- 130g dried tamarind*
- 130g ginger, peeled and finely chopped
- 3 garlic cloves, peeled and cut julienne
- 1 green chilli, finely sliced
- 165g jaggery, chopped*
- 1 teaspoon salt (or to taste)

**MASALA**

- ½ teaspoon mustard seeds
- ½ teaspoon fenugreek seeds
- ½ teaspoon fennel seeds
- ½ teaspoon cumin seeds

**INGREDIENTS FOR TEMPERING/ FINAL FRY/TADKA**

- 1 tablespoon vegetable oil
- ½ teaspoon mustard seeds
- 1 dried red chilli
- 5 curry leaves, shredded

* *Ganapati use dried blocks of tamarind and blocks of jaggery (unrefined palm sugar) that you can find in your local Asian grocers or in some supermarkets.*

**Ganapati's own version of the well-known ginger and tamarind preserve. It'll keep for weeks in the fridge so you can keep going back for more!**

For the masala, dry-roast the mustard, fenugreek, fennel and cumin seeds in a small frying pan until the mustard seeds pop and the other spices darken and become aromatic, then set aside.

Once cool, grind the spices to a powder.

Break the tamarind into pieces into a bowl and soak in 500ml boiling water.

Leave the tamarind to cool slightly and then work with your hands and then with a whisk to mix well.

Sieve the tamarind into a stainless steel saucepan.

Remove the left behind fibres and pulp from the sieve and put back into the bowl with 400ml hot water and repeat the above steps.

Bring the pan to boil and simmer uncovered for about ten minutes until the liquid reduces by about a quarter.

Add the chopped ginger, garlic and the green chilli and continue to simmer briskly, uncovered, for 5-10 minutes.

Add the jaggery and reduce the heat.

Stir until the jaggery has dissolved, then add the powdered masala and salt.

Continue to cook for another 5 minutes, check seasoning and remove from the heat.

In a small frying pan, heat a tablespoon of vegetable oil.

# GAYLORD LAMB SHANK

## SERVED WITH NAAN OR PULAO

**Serves 2**

**INGREDIENTS**

1 teaspoon ginger paste
1 teaspoon garlic paste
2 teaspoons ground cumin
1 teaspoon ground turmeric
Salt
1 teaspoon chilli powder
2 teaspoons fresh lemon juice
100g yoghurt, whisked
2 lamb shanks
50g vegetable oil or clarified butter
2 cinnamon sticks
3 cardamom pods
4 cloves
3 small onions*
3 large ripe tomatoes*
2 bay leaves
2 star anise
¼ mace
2 teaspoons ground coriander
500ml hot water
A few drops of kewra water

**GARNISH**

Fresh coriander leaves
Ginger matchsticks
Green chillies, sliced

* *Both onions and tomatoes need to be turned into a paste separately before cooking. Alternatively, use equal amounts of ready-made onion and tomato pastes*

**The most popular dish at the restaurant, Gaylord's signature lamb shank is a great alternative if you don't fancy a sauce heavy curry dish but still want to enjoy the great flavours they offer. The chefs at Gaylord have worked hard to create this dish and put together a perfect blend of ingredients so that you can replicate the dish at home – though heading to London and trying the real thing couldn't hurt either, could it?**

Mix the ginger and garlic pastes, cumin, turmeric, 1 teaspoon of salt, chilli powder, lemon juice and yoghurt in a large mixing bowl to make a thick paste.

Make small cuts in the lamb shanks and then coat in the paste, then set aside for 2 hours.

Heat the oil in a large saucepan. Add the cinnamon, cardamom and cloves and sauté for 30 seconds.

Add the onion paste and sauté over a medium heat, stirring occasionally until golden brown

Add the turmeric, chilli, bay leaves, star anise, mace, cumin and coriander powders and salt and sauté until the colour starts to change.

Add the tomato paste and stir, then let simmer for 5 minutes.

Add the marinated lamb shanks to the pan and sear over a high heat for 5 minutes, stirring constantly.

Add 500ml of hot water to cover the shanks and bring to a boil. Cover with a lid, simmer, and cook until the lamb is done (approximately 1 hour).

Remove the lid and cook for a further 10 minutes or until the sauce has reduced to the desired consistency and then season to taste with salt.

To finish, add a few drops of kewra water, cover and simmer for a further 15 minutes.

Garnish with fresh coriander leaves, ginger matchsticks and sliced green chillies.

# GAYLORD
## LONDON

**Gaylord is a brand recognised by many as an institution where their parents or grandparents took them out for first taste of the finest curry.**

So say the people behind this, one of the longest-established Indian restaurants in London. It has its roots in 1940s India, but actually opened in the capital back in 1966.

With its smart ivory interior, traditional furniture and original art, the décor is early Elephant Bagger.

And yes, it is exactly the type of place that you could take the heir to your fortune at the end of boarding school term and treat him to a slap-up tea.

Located near Oxford Circus, Gaylord's chief claim to fame is that it was the first restaurant to have a tandoor (a traditional charcoal clay oven), an innovation which caused quite a stir in 1967.

Nowadays of course, practically every local curry house has one. But Gaylord was the first in the field. And it has stuck to its guns over the years, featuring North Indian cuisine of the highest order.

That, along with the elegant surroundings, has made it a magnet for many famous faces from cricket and Bollywood. In an industry where staff turnover is notoriously high, the restaurant's team has remained remarkably stable. Gaylord's head chef has been with them for over 30 years, and the kitchen team has an average of over 15 years working in the restaurant. It still produces the same delectable kebabs and fresh breads that it always has.

**Find them at:**

79-81 Mortimer Street, London, W1W 7SJ

Tel: 020 7636 0808

Email: info@gaylordlondon.com

**www.gaylordlondon.com**

# GRAND TRUNK ROAD

## LONDON

**Rajesh Suri's vision for a restaurant was realised when Grand Trunk Road opened in South Woodford, East London in November 2016.**

The new restaurant was symbolic in more ways than one. It gave Rajesh the opportunity to turn his unusual concept into reality. The theme was to draw its inspiration from the legendary road, which winds along a 1,600-mile passage through distinctive regions of the sub-continent. In the same way, the menu was to represent that journey in culinary style.

But it also reunited him with chef Dayashankar Sharma. The two had previously worked alongside one another at Tamarind, in London's Mayfair and Zaika, in Kensington. Under Suri's management, Tamarind became the first Indian restaurant in Europe to be awarded a Michelin star.

Suri and Sharma share over 58 years of culinary experience, and you might even recognise Suri as a regular face at the Chef's Table on MasterChef: The Professionals. Winner of both Restaurateurs Restaurant of the Year and Restaurant Personality of the Year, Suri is no stranger to being recognised for his work in Indian cuisine. Head chef, Sharma, is no stranger to recognition either, having designed and completed work on events and state banquets, cooking for Presidents, dignitaries and luminaries during his time working at India's Taj Hotel.

Each dish at Grand Trunk Road is a reflection of the diversity that can be found in the towns and cities that sit along the

1,600-mile stretch of road that runs from Bangladesh to Afghanistan. The menu at Grand Trunk Road features the chargrilled delicacies of Peshawar and Rawalpindi, the fried fish of Punjab and the kebabs and biriyanis of Awadhi, with the menu's vegetarian options coming from the region of Varanasi.

Here, the décor matches the menu, the old is mixed in with the new. Traditional Indian wall panels are contrasted with beaten copper hanging lights and exposed brick walls. Sofas and large booths are a far cry from the usual white-linen tablecloths we have grown accustomed to expect when dining at Indian restaurants.

**Find them at:**

219 High Road, London, E18 2PB
Tel: 020 8505 1965
Email: rajesh@gtrrestaurant.co.uk
**www.gtrrestaurant.co.uk**

# HYDERABADI ROYAL LAMB SHANK

## (GREAT WITH STEAMED RICE OR NAAN BREAD)

**Serves 4**

**INGREDIENTS**

4 lamb shanks
4 tablespoons vegetable oil
2 tablespoons fennel seeds
4 medium onions, peeled and sliced
3 tablespoons ginger and garlic paste, freshly ground
1 tablespoon turmeric powder
½ tablespoon chilli powder
1 tablespoon cumin powder
1 tablespoon coriander powder
Salt, to taste
4 tablespoons natural yoghurt
2 litres lamb stock, fat free
½ tablespoon rose water
½ tablespoon kewra water
2 pieces mace
½ tablespoon Kashmiri chilli powder
2 tablespoons shank masala powder*

***SHANK MASALA INGREDIENTS**

Fennel seeds, cloves, Kashmiri chilli, cardamom, cinnamon, clove, mace
(Equal quantity of all ingredients but adjust according to personal cooking methods)

**One of the best-selling dishes at Grand Trunk Road, this dish is perfect for all meat lovers. First created in 1600 by chefs at a royal palace, this slow-cooked lamb shank with browned onion, garlic and yoghurt, complete with freshly ground spices is the perfect dish to pull out at your next dinner party.**

Rinse the lamb shank under cold water.

Heat oil in a large saucepan for 30 seconds.

Add the fennel seeds and then add the onion and brown it over a medium heat, stirring occasionally.

Add the lamb shank to the pan and cook over a high heat for 5 minutes, stirring constantly.

Add the ginger and garlic paste and stir well for 2 minutes.

Add the turmeric, chilli, cumin and coriander powders, add salt and cook for five minutes.

Add the yoghurt and sauté for 5 minutes over a high heat.

Add the lamb stock, stir and simmer for 5 minutes until the oil separates from the sauce.

Add enough water to cover the shank and bring to boil, cover with the lid and let it simmer until the lamb is cooked (approximately 1 hour).

Remove the saucepan from the heat and remove cooked shank from the sauce.

Strain the cooked sauce and cook over the heat for a further 10 minutes or until reduced to desired consistency, check seasoning.

Blend the remaining sauce into a smooth paste.

To finish, add the cooked lamb shank back into the sauce, cover and simmer for 15 minutes, then add the rose water and kewra water.

Serve.

# MASALA PRAWNS

**Serves 2**

**INGREDIENTS**

500g queen prawns
50g butter
1 onion, coarsely chopped
1 lemon
½ red bell pepper, coarsely chopped
½ green bell pepper, coarsely chopped
½ yellow bell pepper, coarsely chopped
½ orange bell pepper, coarsely chopped
4 tablespoons coriander, chopped
2 teaspoons vegetable oil
½ teaspoon cumin seeds

**MASALA INGREDIENTS**

2 onions, finely chopped
2 green chillies, finely chopped
2 tomatoes, finely chopped
4 teaspoons vegetable oil
2 teaspoons garlic and ginger paste*
1 teaspoon tomato paste
1 teaspoon cumin seeds
1 teaspoon cumin seeds
¼ teaspoon coriander powder
¼ teaspoon turmeric powder
Chilli powder, to taste
Salt, to taste

**A classic Indian masala dish featuring staple North Indian ingredients and spices including tomatoes, onions and chillies. This dish is quick and easy to prepare and is extremely versatile; simply swap the prawns for a protein of your choice and you'll have a delicious curry to suit every occasion. Aromatic coconut rice makes a perfect accompaniment.**

### Masala sauce

Add the oil to a heavy-based pan.

When the oil is hot, add the cumin seeds.

Add the chopped onions and chillies and cook on a low heat until the onions turn a golden brown.

Add the coriander, turmeric and chilli powders and the salt to taste (a splash of water can be added to aid the cooking of the onions and the blending of the spices).

Add the garlic and ginger paste and cook for a further 3 minutes.

Add the chopped tomatoes and tomato paste and cook on a low heat until the oil starts to separate and the masala is well blended.

Remove the pan from the heat and set to one side

### Prawns

Heat the butter and oil in a pan

Sear the prawns on a high heat for 1-2 minutes, then remove from the pan and set to one side.

Add the onion and peppers to the pan and stir-fry.

Once the onions begin to brown, add the cooked masala sauce and mix well.

Add the prawns and toss on a high heat until cooked through.

Garnish with coriander, lemon juice and toasted cumin seeds.

Serve hot with steamed rice or coconut rice*

* to make coconut rice – replace half of the required quantity of water with coconut milk, cover the rice with lots of curry leaves when steaming for added depth and flavour; remove them before serving.

# HAANDI

## LONDON

**The Mall in Nairobi, Kenya, was Haandi's home when the doors of its first branch opened in 1991. Having arrived in Kenya with an enviable pedigree, Pradeep Mullick had honed his skills in the kitchens of world class hotels such as The Sheraton and The Taj. His experience combined with that of Ray Bhangra is what brought Haandi to life, and in 2000, following the success that their first branch had seen, Ray arrived in London to celebrate the millennium with the opening of Haandi, Knightsbridge.**

Tucked away on a quiet street near Harrods, Haandi is a different proposition from the prim and proper restaurants that overwhelm the area. Specialising in North Indian Frontier cuisine, Haandi serve customers a wide selection of seafood, poultry, meat and vegetarian dishes, ensuring that that spices and herbs used in each dish are selected not only for their flavours but also for the health benefits they each contain. Haandi do their best to stay true to the spirit of great Indian cooking, preparing each masala fresh every day, and each chef hired by the restaurant is trained by Pradeep himself to make sure that they understand Haandi's ethos and the importance of authenticity.

Haandi see a wide range of customers coming through their doors, from tourists and shoppers to locals and East African expatriates who come to enjoy some of the dishes they've tried at Haandi's first home in Nairobi. You don't need to visit the restaurant to enjoy the food that they offer, however. Haandi's portable Tandoor means that the food and service you would enjoy in Knightsbridge can be brought directly to you. Haandi can cater for events whether there are 50 or 1000 guests attending, whether it be a barbeque, champagne reception or a wedding; and they ensure no matter the size of the party, that the event is meticulously organised and fuss-free so that the organiser can sit back, relax and enjoy their experience.

**Find them at:**

7 Cheval Place, Knightsbridge,
London, SW7 1EW
Tel: 020 7823 7373
Email: info@haandirestaurants.com
**www.haandirestaurants.com**

# INDIAN TIFFIN ROOM

## CHESHIRE, MANCHESTER, LEEDS

**Influenced by all regions of India and the street food served within them, Indian Tiffin Room offer an amalgamation of various regional dishes across their three restaurants. Believing that a lot of curry houses are still serving their customers food overwhelmed by oil and spice, Indian Tiffin Room are instead focusing on the nuances of flavour within their dishes.**

Indian Tiffin Room opened in 2013 with the aim of serving their customers what they felt was missing from Indian restaurants the UK. Starting in Cheadle with their 30-cover restaurant, they've since added two more to the family in Manchester and Leeds, and are serving up dishes such as dosas, thali, chaats, kebabs and Indo-Chinese food amongst many more. Their group head chef, Selvan, has been with the company since day one and still creates the menu while overseeing the quality standards across the chain.

With a reasonably-priced menu, Indian Tiffin Room are not striving to become one of the new fine dining Indian restaurants on the scene, and are instead more than happy to be an accessible destination. Welcoming students, professionals and families through their doors, the Indian Tiffin Room restaurants are friendly and casual, and this is reflected by the interiors of each location.

Each restaurant has its own stand-out features... Cheadle with its bamboo ceilings, Manchester with its shipping containers and Leeds with its arches, reflecting the colonial

past of India. Each restaurant is different but they are of one mind on the thing of most importance, and that is the food that they serve.

And watch this space. Indian Tiffin room are planning six or seven new restaurants in the North West in the coming years.

**Find them at:**

2 Chapel Street, Cheadle, Cheshire, SK8 1BR
Tel: 0161 491 2020
Email: info@indiantiffinroom.com

2 Isabella Banks Street, First Street
Manchester, M15 4RL
Tel: 0161 228 1000
Email: infomanchester@indiantiffinroom.com

31-32 Park Row (entrance on Greek Street), Leeds
Tel: 0113 397 2000
**www.indiantiffinroom.com**

# BEETROOT SHAMI KEBAB

**Serves 4**

**INGREDIENTS**

200g beetroot
½ tablespoon cumin
1 red onion, chopped
2 tablespoons ginger and garlic paste
1 tablespoon coriander powder
1 teaspoon chilli powder
Salt, to taste
100g potatoes
2 tablespoons plain flour
100ml water
100g breadcrumbs

**This dish is based on the classic street food dish, Shami Kebab. More commonly a meat-based dish, the team at Indian Tiffin Room have created their own vegetarian-friendly version by substituting the meat with beetroot, giving the kebabs a new and fresh flavour.**

Wash, peel and grate the beetroot. Squeeze the juice into a mixing bowl.

Heat oil in a deep pan, then add the cumin seeds and chopped onions, sautéing until the onions turn a light brown.

Add the ginger and garlic paste to the pan, then add the coriander and chilli powders. Add the salt and sauté for one minute.

Add the grated beetroot and sauté for a few minutes until the beetroot is half cooked, then cool the mixture down.

Boil the potatoes in a saucepan, then once boiled, grate into the mixture.

Divide the mixture into equal portions and shape them into balls/patties.

In a bowl, mix the plain flour together with 100ml of water.

Heat oil in a deep pan, dip the patties into the flour mixture to form a thin wet coating over the patties, and then coat in the breadcrumbs and deep fry until a golden brown.

Serve hot with tomato ketchup or mint and tamarind chutney.

# BHARWAN MIRCH MALABAR

**Serves 2-3**

**INGREDIENTS**

Sauce

1 teaspoon black mustard seeds
6-8 curry leaves, chiffonade
2 teaspoon rapeseed oil
1 medium onion, finely diced
1 tomato, finely diced
½ teaspoon cumin powder
½ teaspoon turmeric powder
½ teaspoon madras curry powder
½ teaspoon mild Kashmiri chilli powder
1 teaspoon water
400ml coconut milk
1 teaspoon lemon juice
½ teaspoon salt
1 teaspoon fresh coriander, finely chopped

**POTATO STUFFING**

6 baby peppers
1 large potato
1 teaspoon salt
½ teaspoon turmeric
½ teaspoon chilli powder
½ teaspoon lemon juice (or to taste)
1 teaspoon cumin powder
1 teaspoon kasuri methi (dried fenugreek leaves)

**CASSAVA CROQUETTES**

1 small cassava, boiled and mashed
1 teaspoon salt
½ teaspoon chilli powder
2 teaspoons mild red chilli, finely chopped
½ teaspoon lemon juice to taste
2 teaspoons cornflour

**GARNISH**

3 handfuls rice noodles
40-50 pomegranate kernels
10 curry leaves, fried
Fresh coriander, chopped

**Vegetarian dishes are usually the last to be developed in a restaurant. However, Lilu have paid special attention to this dish and have been working on it over time in a bid to inspire even the biggest of carnivores to give the flavours of vegetarian food a try.**

To make the sauce, heat oil in a pan and add the mustard seeds and curry leaves and allow them to pop.

Add the onions and tomatoes, stir and soften the onions for 1-2 minutes and then add dry spices and water.

Cook out the raw spices until all the onions have become translucent with a yellow colour from the turmeric, approximately 3-4 minutes.

Add the coconut milk, mix through and then cook for 20 minutes on a low-medium heat, until the oil is starting to separate from the sauce.

Taste for seasoning and add lemon juice and salt.

Fry the baby peppers by cutting off the tops and removing the seeds.

To make the potato stuffing for the baby pepper, mix all ingredients for the potato stuffing and then warm through in a saucepan. Check seasoning and then stuff peppers and keep warm in warm oven.

Make the cassava croquettes by mixing all remaining ingredients well and rolling into small golf ball shapes – dust with corn flour and fry in oil heated to 175°C.

Fry the rice noodles.

To serve, place a base of sauce on a plate, then add the cassava croquettes (cut into two) in the centre of the plate. Put two stuffed baby peppers on the plate and add the rice noodles to the centre and garnish with a handful of fried rice noodles, 8-10 pomegranate kernels, 3-4 fried curry leaves and the freshly chopped coriander.

# LILU
## LEICESTER

**The hashtag says it all. Lilu director Pratik Master believes that as a nation we have come to associate Indian food with the kind of fare we're accustomed to finding at the local takeaway – and because of that, we're missing out on some intriguing cuisine.**

So his statement is a bold one – neatly summed up as #notjustacurry.

With a team like he has assembled at Lilu, Pratik is certainly in a position to back up his claim.

Since opening five years ago in 2013, Lilu's team has grown to include head chef Amardeep Singh Anand, a quarter-finalist on MasterChef – The Professionals and winner of Asian Chef of the Year 2012. Chef Singh has worked in catering, hotels and five-star resorts in India. Pratik allows chef Singh creative licence in his kitchen, where he brings unique dishes to life and demonstrates different styles of regional cooking, while still ensuring a British influence can be seen.

The result is a menu which features the likes of Soft Shell Crab and Rack of Lamb. While these may not appear to be traditional Indian dishes, they nevertheless reflect authentic Indian flavours. Pratik believes that Lilu represents a generation of British Indians who grew up having everyday curry at home but look for something different from a restaurant.

While many Indian restaurants believe in function over form, at Lilu presentation is just as important as the flavours on the plate. And an Indian restaurant really needs to be distinctive in order to win acclaim in its home city of Leicester, which boasts a huge number of eateries.

It may not be as simple as a choice between quality and quantity. But if restaurant owners like Pratik continue to lead the way, the landscape surrounding Indian cuisine in Britain is undoubtedly changing.

**Find them at:**

76 Highcross Street, Leicester, LE1 4NN

Tel: 0116 262 3119

Email: reservations@lilurestaurant.co.uk

**lilurestaurant.co.uk**

# MASALA WALA CAFÉ

## LONDON

**As they near their fourth year of business, mother and daughter team Nabeela Muqadiss and Saima Arshad's restaurant, Masala Wala Café, is going from strength to strength. Having convinced her mother to open a restaurant serving her Pakistani home cooking, Saima uses her customer service expertise to run the business side of things, and ensure that she's always putting a smile on the faces of their customers.**

The menu at Masala Wala Café may appear small at first, but it changes on a rotational basis to work with the seasonal British produce they use, meaning there are plenty of dishes to try as the year moves on. You'll definitely want to come back each season once you've tried even just one of the dishes on offer at Masala Wala Café; as their food is inspired by the Punjab region which extends over North India and Pakistan. The flavours they use are robust and unforgiving, but also simple enough that you won't feel like there's too much happening on your plate.

The mum and daughter duo use traditional, labour intensive methods that have been used by mothers across the subcontinent for longer than anyone can remember. A world away from the typical British curry house, Masala Wala Café welcome any and everyone through their doors, from South Asians wanting a taste of home to well-travelled locals and regulars.

Masala Wala Café proves that more women are successfully stepping forward and starting to diversify this male-dominated industry, but Nabeela and Saima are well aware that there is still a lot of work to be done. Indian restaurants are closing down due to chef shortages, so the pair believe the industry should be looking outside of the box, and supporting women and chefs beyond the subcontinent.

**Find them at:**

5 Brockley Cross, London, SE4 2AB

Tel: 020 3659 4055

Email: hello@masalawalacafe.co.uk

**www.masalawalacafe.co.uk**

# GAJAR KA HALWA

**Serves 8-19**

**INGREDIENTS**

10 green cardamom pods
Butter, for frying
1kg carrots, peeled and grated
160g condensed milk
130g brown demerara sugar
½ teaspoon nutmeg
Handful crushed pistachios
100g unsalted butter

Gajar Ka Halwa is a sweet carrot pudding, and while it's a dessert made from a vegetable, you'll be amazed at how much it resembles a rich sticky toffee pudding-like texture and flavour. This dish is an example of true Punjabi indulgence and it's just as moreish as any other sweet dessert!

De-shell the cardamom and crush in a pestle and mortar or coffee grinder until it becomes a powder.

In a deep pan, fry the cardamom powder in some butter over a medium heat, then add the grated carrot and stir continuously.

Cook until the carrots are softened and the moisture has dried out (approximately 20 minutes).

Add the condensed milk and bring to boil over a high heat, stirring through, and then bring back to medium heat until the condensed milk has evaporated.

Add the sugar and nutmeg and stir until it has dissolved.

When ready, the mixture should be moist but all of the condensed milk should have absorbed.

Serve warm and garnish with the crushed pistachios.

# JHINGA HARA MASALA KING PRAWNS

**Serves 4**

INGREDIENTS

12 king prawns
10g ginger and garlic paste
1 teaspoon lemon juice
1 teaspoon oil
20g yoghurt
½ teaspoon garam masala (or more to taste)
2 tablespoons coriander powder
50g mint sauce
Salt, to taste

HARA MASALA PASTE

5 bunches fresh coriander
2 bunches fresh mint
250g green chillies
250ml olive oil

MemSaab's masala prawn recipe is a favourite among their diners. These grilled king prawns are marinated in fresh mint, coriander and green chillies (for a little extra kick) and are the perfect option for when you're feeling peckish but don't want to be weighed down by a heavy, overly saucy dish.

Chop the fresh coriander, mint and green chillies, then add the olive oil and blend/liquidise to create a hara masala paste.

Add the hara masala paste to a large bowl and add the remaining ingredients except for the prawns.

Mix the ingredients together well, and then stir in the raw prawns.

Cover and leave in the fridge for 8-24 hours.

Once the prawns have marinated for long enough, preheat your grill to a high heat.

Place the prawns on a wire rack in a grill pan and heat for approximately 6 minutes, turning halfway through.

Remove from the heat and serve immediately with vegetables or salad.

# MEMSAAB
## NOTTINGHAM

**MemSaab was the first restaurant in the East Midlands to be awarded two AA rosettes for culinary excellence, the first of a long list of accolades.**

Among them are the British Curry Awards Best Indian Restaurant in the Midlands, Nottingham Evening Post's Best Indian Restaurant and runner-up for Best Restaurant in The Observer's Food Monthly Awards four times.

The interior at MemSaab combines traditional Indian craftsmanship with modern Indian art, capturing the essence of India while placing the restaurant firmly in the 21st century.

It's not every restaurant that has Indian head massage on the menu, but an invigorating hands-on experience awaits partygoers.

Host your party here and you'll get to choose between four menus or even create your own bespoke menu with their team. Unique flower design, head massage and mehndi (henna) can be arranged as part of the package.

Between the chefs at MemSaab there's a strong knowledge of regional Indian, Pakistani and modern Indian cuisine, with each chef implementing their own individual style in the kitchen.

The innovative menu features dishes at all price points, so it will suit all preferences and budgets. They've a wide range of options, from their Venison Kebabs and Tandoori Ostrich starters to their indulgent main courses of Dumpukht Lamb Loin, served with masala mashed potato and saffron sauce, and their Pan Fried Seabass with spiced ratatouille and coconut tamarind jus.

For those struggling to decide what to order, owner Amita Sawhney is always on hand to recommend dishes. MemSaab can comfortably accommodate up to 200 diners and has two private dining rooms offering flexible seating from 8 to 60.

**Find them at:**
12-14 Maid Marian Way, Nottingham, NG1 6HS
Tel: 0115 957 0009
Email: contact@mem-saab.co.uk
**www.mem-saab.co.uk**

# THE MINT ROOM

## BRISTOL, BATH

**The Mint Room restaurants have made themselves at home in two of South-West England's major cities. Originally starting out in Bath, Mint Room found themselves immensely popular with locals and visitors to the historical Roman city, and there followed a second branch in Bristol.**

While many restaurants might stick to what they know when expanding, Mint Room decided they wanted to distance themselves from their original restaurant and serve a slightly different menu in an alternative setting.

Mint Room Bristol's menu is made up of both traditional and contemporary Indian dishes. Their Balchao Lobster and Goan Kekada are examples of how well their executive chef Saravanan Nambirajan plays with flavour combinations, and their Tour of India tasting menu is a guaranteed crowd-pleaser, featuring seven courses that will take you on a culinary journey through the subcontinent. This can be paired with their wine flight which has been designed to perfectly complement each course.

The menu at Mint Room Bath has more of a traditional, homely feel to it. Full of classics we all know and love, and some real authentic dishes that we may have heard of but haven't quite got around to trying, like their King Prawn Moilee or the Kokum Fish, or even Paneer Tikka. Mint Room Bath's menu is full of gluten-free and vegetarian dishes, so there's plenty of choice for everyone.

The restaurants themselves are almost as visually stunning as the food they serve. Displaying the visual and cultural contrasts between Britain and India, the Bristol restaurant has exposed brickwork and aubergine red walls, adorned with large, sculptural Indian mirrors.

Looking like Mint Room Bristol's more modern older sister, Mint Room Bath has a sleek dining area and a heated, open-air champagne bar. They've created the perfect environment for a nice meal out as well as a great place to head to for some pre- or post-dinner drinks (weather permitting, of course, as although we've been blessed with their cuisine, we've not quite caught on to how to bring over the sun!).

**Find them at:**

12-16 Clifton Road, Clifton, Bristol, BS8 1AF

Tel: 0117 329 1300

Email: bristol@mintroom.co.uk

**www.mintroombristol.co.uk**

Longmead Gospel Hall, Lower Bristol Road, Bath, BA2 3EB

Tel: 01225 446656

Email: bath@mintroom.co.uk

**www.mintroombath.co.uk**

# KADDAI MUTTA MEEN KOZHAMBU
## (STUFFED SALMON FISH CURRY)

**Serves 5**

INGREDIENTS

STUFFED SALMON BALLS

10 quail eggs
1kg minced salmon
50g coriander, finely chopped
6 green chillies
50g ginger
3 stalks lemongrass
10 fresh lemon leaves
2 teaspoons turmeric powder
Salt, to taste

SAUCE

2 teaspoons mustard seeds
1 teaspoon cumin seeds
1 teaspoon fenugreek seeds
2 sprigs curry leaves
250g onion, chopped
25g ginger, julienned
50g garlic, sliced
500g tomato, diced
1 teaspoon turmeric powder
2 teaspoons chilli powder
3 teaspoons coriander powder
Salt, to taste
200ml tamarind pulp
150ml water
250ml coconut milk

Kaddai Mutta Meen Kozhambu is one of the most famous and traditional seafood sauces used in South Indian cooking, especially in the region of Tamil Nadu. At Mint Room, they've teamed the sauce with salmon stuffed with quail eggs, giving the dish a bit of a twist and infusing the sauce with a bit of modernity, giving their customers a dish so beautifully presented that they don't want to ruin it by cutting into it! One bite though, and that all changes...

Parboil the quail eggs, peel and set aside.

Add the minced salmon, coriander, chillies, ginger, lemongrass, lemon leaves, turmeric and salt to a mixing bowl and mix well.

Once combined, divide the mixture into ten equal portions and stuff with the quail eggs, making them into even ball shape and set aside.

Heat some oil in a saucepan, add the mustard seeds, cumin, fenugreek seeds and curry leaves and let the mixture sizzle in the oil for about a minute.

Add the chopped onion, ginger and garlic, then stir gently until colour turns transparent.

Add the diced tomatoes and cook on a low heat for ten minutes, gradually adding the turmeric, chilli and coriander powders and salt

Add the tamarind pulp and 150ml water and bring to the boil, leave for 10-15 minutes until the flavour of the tamarind dissipates.

Blend the sauce well and strain.

Add the fine sauce to a wide saucepan and simmer on a low heat.

Add the coconut milk and check that the seasoning is to your taste, keeping the saucepan on a low heat to ensure the milk doesn't curdle.

Gradually place the stuffed salmon balls into the sauce and leave to cook for about 7-8 minutes.

Remove the cooked salmon balls from the sauce and cut in half so that the eggs are visible.

Serve with steamed white rice or Indian steamed rice cakes.

# TANDOORI VEGETABLES

**Serves 4**

**INGREDIENTS**

4 carrots, cut into thin batons
4 parsnips, cut into thin batons
1 small turnip, diced (approx. 1cm cubed)
4 courgettes, diced (approx. 4cm cubed)
2 plum tomatoes, quartered
1 leek, chopped
1 red pepper, diced (approx. 4cm cubed)
1 green pepper, diced (approx. 4cm cubed)
4 shallots, peeled and quartered
4 garlic cloves

**MARINADE**

3 tablespoons natural yoghurt
2 tablespoons tandoori paste
1 tablespoon Harissa paste
1 tablespoon mustard or olive oil
Juice of 1 lemon
2 green chillies, crushed
½ tablespoon cumin, roasted
1 tablespoon black peppercorns, cracked
1 teaspoon garam masala
1 tablespoon salt
½ tablespoon red chilli powder

Whether you want to follow Mother India's recipe exactly, or whether you like to get adventurous in the kitchen and add your own personal touch to your dishes, this recipe is simple and easy to follow. You can use the veg as per this recipe, or add in or take out as many as you like, just make sure you know how long each vegetable needs in the oven!

Preheat the oven to 200°C.

Add all of the ingredients for the marinade to a large bowl and mix together.

Add the vegetables to the marinade and ensure they're all evenly coated.

Transfer the vegetables to large oven tray and cover with foil.

Place the tray into the oven for about 35 minutes or until all of the vegetables are nice and tender.

Serve.

# MOTHER INDIA
## GLASGOW, EDINBURGH

Mother India's journey began with the their first restaurant in Glasgow in 1990, with the simple idea of serving customers authentic Indian home cooking in a restaurant setting. Fast forward, and there are now two Mother India restaurants in Scotland, with the second making its home in Edinburgh. Both aim to offer their diners a casual experience, aspiring to give them the best of Indian subcontinental food at affordable prices.

At Mother India they work hard to not only maintain, but also to improve upon, the high standards that they set themselves and that their customers have come to expect over time. Their chefs are constantly working to expand and refresh their menus, while retaining their established favourites and offering a range of specials created with the best seasonal products and freshest ingredients they can source.

The menu here encourages diners to try something new, as their extensive menu is comprised of smaller portions, a sort of Indian twist on tapas. At Mother India they believe in 'trying a little and tasting a lot', and creating a shared experience for their guests. Why limit yourself to just one dish when you can try a few and perhaps stumble onto a new favourite?

Mother India endeavour to make sure that the dining rooms at their restaurants are unique and interesting spaces, so that customers feel comfortable and find themselves not only excited for the meal they're about to eat, but also leave asking questions about India and its culture.

All of this put together seems to be a winning recipe for Mother India, as on any given night, you can expect to see the restaurant filled with food lovers from around the world, mixing happily with regulars and local first timers.

**Find them at:**
1355 Argyle Street, Glasgow, G3 8AD
Tel: 0141 339 9145

3-5 Infirmary Street, Edinburgh, EH1 1LT
Tel: 0131 524 9801
**www.motherindia.co.uk**

# MUGHLI
## MANCHESTER, KNUTSFORD

**A second-generation family restaurant serving home-style 'Indian Soul Food' and small plates, Mughli opened on Manchester's 'Curry Mile' in 1991. The family's late father was behind the original restaurant, but today it is run by the four Mughli brothers, with their mother there to help them along the way by approving each menu they've launched.**

Mughli's cuisine is inspired by the historic Mughal Empire which wielded such influence in the North-West regions of India. They take great inspiration from Persian and Central Asian cuisine, where the Turco-Mongol Mughal rulers originally hailed from, so expect to see some unusual dishes on the menu. The drinks list at Mughli is also something out of the ordinary, featuring Indian-inspired cocktails and house-infused G&Ts that perfectly complement their cuisine.

The flavours that their chefs create are not confined within the walls of their two restaurants however, as Mughli have hosted pop-ups across the country at locations including Selfridges and at street food events such as B.Eat Street. They've also collaborated with acclaimed chefs such as David Gale and Ernst van Zyl and have found themselves becoming a favourite of UK and international celebrities.

Mughli's large group of regular customers rave about the food and the service they receive each and every time they pay them a visit, and due to the popularity of the restaurant online and among critics, Mughli have seen a great deal of visitors come from outside of Manchester and its suburbs to see for themselves what all the fuss is about. They've even been named one of Manchester's Best Restaurants by The Telegraph and BBC Good Food Guide.

The team at Mughli have worked hard throughout the years to create a quality-led brand which remains loved by their customers, and they're looking forward to their bright future. They'll soon be launching their own cookbook so you'll be able to attempt to recreate the dishes you love in your own home.

**Find them at:**

Charcoal Pit, 30 Wilmslow Road,
Manchester, M14 5TQ
Tel: 0161 248 0900
Email: manchester@mughli.com

Bar & Kitchen
44 King Street, Knutsford, WA16 6DT
Tel: 01565 631010
Email: knutsford@mughli.com
**www.mughli.com**

# SALMON TIKKA

**Serves 4**

**INGREDIENTS**

2 tablespoons mustard oil
Pinch mustard seeds
1 tablespoon ginger, garlic and coriander paste
1 teaspoon green mint chutney
½ teaspoon red chilli powder
½ teaspoon turmeric powder
Juice of half a lemon
Salt, to taste
2 salmon fillets, skin on

**Although not native to India, salmon is a great meaty, oily fish which perfectly absorbs and works with this quick and easy family recipe. With the addition of just a few spices, you can add a real Indian twist to what could usually be quite a plain dish. Mughli's recipe doesn't take long to prepare, and is great when cooked in the oven, best when gently smoked over a BBQ alongside a fresh, citrusy salad on a summer's day.**

Heat the oil in a pan, then add the mustard seeds until they begin to crackle.

Remove the pan from the heat, and add the mustard seeds into a large mixing bowl, then add the remainder of the ingredients except for the salmon, and mix well.

Skin side up, cut through the salmon fillets slightly with a sharp knife to allow the marinade to penetrate.

Add the salmon fillets to the marinade, ensuring that they are fully coated, then cover the bowl and leave to marinate for at least 2 hours.

Preheat the oven to 200°C.

Place the salmon, skin side down, on a lightly greased baking dish and bake for between 12-15 minutes (depending on the thickness of the fillets).

Serve.

# RAJMA GALOUTI KEBABS

**Serves 3**

**INGREDIENTS**

180g red kidney beans (soaked for 8 hours)
5 cloves
Cinnamon stick, approx. 4 inches
1 black cardamom pod
2 green cardamom pods
¼ teaspoon caraway seeds
½ teaspoon poppy seeds
8 cashew nuts
½ teaspoon red chilli powder
Salt, to taste
Oil for frying
Yoghurt, as required

**Kidney beans are an ingredient frequently used in India, and this recipe helps to introduce protein-rich foods to the diet. A great dish to go with a pint as the kebabs complement the frothiness wonderfully. Rich in varied flavours, the taste and texture of these kebabs are a perfect filler while you're waiting for your main course.**

Boil the soaked kidney beans in a pan until soft.
Once soft, mash until the beans blend together .
Dry roast the cloves, cinnamon, black and green cardamom pods, caraway and poppy seeds in a pan until fragrant.
Add the cashew nuts and roast until brown.
Allow to cool and then grind into a powder.
Mix the mashed kidney beans, red chilli powder, salt and combine with the ground spices.
Divide the mixture into equal portions with damp hands and shape into tikkis.
Heat oil in a wok and shallow fry the tikkis, until both sides are golden brown.
Serve hot with yoghurt and coriander chutney.*

*To make your own coriander chutney, simply combine coriander with some groundnuts, salt, sugar, lemon and green chillies and grind together.

# PILAU

## LONDON

**Young restaurant entrepreneur George Pitkeathley is the man behind PILAU. And presumably he's the man who decided to have the name set in capitals – a canny move, as it certainly grabs the attention.**

Having started out on the street food scene, he opened the first PILAU restaurant on Goodge Street in 2016 and there's now an additional site in Soho. Both restaurants were opened before George's 24th birthday, and there are now plans to open a third.

His entrepreneurial talent has not gone unnoticed. George received a 30 Under 30 Award and was crowned Young Achiever by The Prince's Trust Foundation.

PILAU is described as a fast-casual dining experience, and unlike other Indian restaurants they're a predominantly lunchtime eatery. At PILAU, the aim is to provide the tastiest food possible, every day, to every customer. George, menu developer Hetal and the team at PILAU are immensely proud of the food they offer. They use traditional flavours in a contemporary format and the menu allows you to customise your order. Customers are able to choose either a wrap, rice bowl or salad bowl and then decide whether they'd like butter chicken, lamb and bone marrow or paneer. With such a young owner and team, it's no wonder that PILAU is such a modern and fun restaurant, even down to their playlist.

The team at PILAU believe that the general standard of Indian food is improving on a daily basis, and together

they're constantly trying out the latest Indian restaurants and are often inspired by how much the sector has developed over the last five years.

While PILAU are focused on providing the best food and experience possible, it's not only their customers that benefit when they dine with them. Through their Feed Yourself – Feed a Child campaign, PILAU donate a mid-morning meal to a child in India every time someone eats at one of their restaurants. So far they've donated thousands of meals, but their main goal is to feed a billion children through this project.

**Find them at:**

34 Goodge Street, Fitzrovia, London, W1T 2QL

22 Noel Street, Soho, London, W1F 8GS
Tel: 07954 576380
Email: george@pilau.co
**www.pilaurestaurant.co.uk**

# PIPAL TREE

## BRISTOL

**This husband and wife-owned restaurant has been making many friends in its first year in business. And in a very short space of time it's even clocked up a few milestones.**

Take the remarkable achievement of reaching the coveted top spot on Tripadvisor – and that a mere four months after it opened in the heart of Easton, Bristol. And yes, it still occupies the summit.

Not bad for a family-run restaurant, presided over by husband and wife Kirpal Singh and Kulwinder Kaul. Their menu is made up of authentic Punjabi and British-Punjabi fusion dishes, with each item on the menu inspired by three generations of their own family recipes.

Pipal Tree want all of their customers to feel comfortable when they dine with them, and they work hard to ensure that people from all walks of life are able to find something on the menu that suits their tastes and needs. An impressive one-third of their menu caters to vegans and vegetarians, and they also offer gluten-free dishes and even a kids' menu for the little ones.

While the majority of the menu demonstrates a marriage between Punjabi and British-Punjabi cuisines, the brunch menu looks a little bit like a divorce, demonstrating just how different the cuisines can be, featuring traditional Punjabi breakfast dishes such as Punjabi Tharka Beans alongside the great British staple, the fry-up.

With the number of their regular diners continuing to grow, Kirpal is using his 20 years of experience as a senior chef to ensure that the menu at Pipal Tree is always evolving. They want to make sure that the quality of their menu remains at the same high level, yet that they are able to provide their customers with new and exciting dishes that they won't have seen before, and will make them want to keep coming back to try out something different. Kirpal and Kulwinder consider themselves true Bristolians, and they want to continue to give back to the community that has given so much to themselves and their young family.

**Find them at:**

28 Chelsea Road, Bristol, BS5 6AF

Tel: 0117 955 8820

Email: pipaltree123@hotmail.com

**www.pipaltreerestaurant.com**

# FUSION MURGA BREAST

**Serves 1**

INGREDIENTS
1 chicken breast
10ml olive oil
½ pepper, sliced
1 red onion
3 cherry tomatoes
2 Portobello mushrooms, sliced
75ml red wine
50ml whipping cream
2 large King Edward potatoes

TANDOORI PASTE
1 teaspoon salt
1 teaspoon cayenne pepper
1 teaspoon chilli powder
1 teaspoon turmeric
1 teaspoon fennel
1 teaspoon cumin
1 teaspoon paprika
1 teaspoon yoghurt
1 teaspoon fresh lemon juice
2 teaspoons olive oil
½ teaspoon garlic paste
½ teaspoon ginger paste
1g fresh coriander, chopped

A combination of British and Punjabi flavours and techniques, this dish has been a staple within the Singh household for over 40 years, and for most of this time the recipe remained a family secret. Today the secret is out, and the dish is a well-loved favourite on the Pipal Tree menu. Once you've allowed yourself the 24 hours for the tandoori paste to combine perfectly, this dish comes together in under half an hour.

Combine all of the ingredients for the tandoori paste in a large bowl.

Rub and mix the ingredients together thoroughly to make a paste.

Rub the paste very well into the chicken breast and place the chicken breast into the fridge for a minimum of 24 hours.

Once the chicken breast has been allowed to marinade in the paste for at least 24 hours, tenderise the chicken breast so that it is of an even thickness.

Add a splash of oil into a hot pan.

Place the chicken breast in the pan and cook for 3 minutes.

# WATTANA & FLOWER (PEA & CAULIFLOWER CURRY)

## (VEGAN, GLUTEN FREE & NUT FREE)

**Serves 4**

**INGREDIENTS**

100ml sunflower oil
1 teaspoon cumin seeds
1 teaspoon brown mustard seeds
½ teaspoon asafoetida
1 medium-sized cauliflower, cut into 1cm pieces
1 teaspoon turmeric
1 tablespoon ground coriander
1 ½ teaspoon salt
1 teaspoon sugar
75ml boiling water (if using fresh peas)
400g peas (fresh or frozen*)
1 medium tomato, finely chopped
1 large handful fresh coriander, roughly chopped

**FOR THE MASALA**

3-6 fresh green chillies (ideally Kenyan), trimmed but not de-seeded
5cm root ginger, peeled and roughly chopped
Pinch of salt

* *If using frozen peas, the chef recommends petit pois as they are smaller and sweeter than ordinary garden peas.*

**This dish appeared on Prashad's very first restaurant menu, and seven years on it's still a firm favourite of their customers. The combination of the cauliflower and the peas is characteristic of traditional Gujarati cooking as they love good textures and a little bit of sweetness in their cuisine.**

To make the masala, crush the chillies and ginger together with a pinch of salt with a pestle and mortar (or blender) to make a fine paste.
Heat the oil in a large thick-based frying pan over a medium heat for 30 seconds before adding the cumin and mustard seeds.
When the mustard seeds start to pop, reduce to a low heat and stir in the asafoetida (heating the spices in this order is essential to the flavour of the dish).
Use a wooden or heatproof plastic spoon to stir in the cauliflower, return the heat to medium, then stir in the masala paste, turmeric, ground coriander, salt, sugar and boiling water (if using fresh peas).
Cover the pan and leave to cook for 8-10 minutes, stirring every few minutes
Stir in the peas and tomato, re-cover and cook for a further 3-5 minutes before removing from the heat.

# PRASHAD
## DRIGHLINGTON

**In 1992, Kaushy Patel converted what was once a laundrette into a local deli; 12 years later it changed once again, this time becoming the restaurant we now know as Prashad. Today, 14 years later still, the restaurant is run by his son Bobby and her daughter-in-law and head chef, Minal.**

Following their appearance on Gordon Ramsay's Best Restaurant, Prashad have gained a national customer base and are now recognised as one of the jewels of Yorkshire. Prashad's menu is strictly vegetarian and offers their customers a wealth of choices inspired by classical Gujarati cooking, fused with modern British techniques. Minal grew up in a traditional Gujarati village and would often have neighbours bringing their ingredients to her family home to watch her prepare their food. Having only moved to the UK in 2004 when she married Bobby, Minal learned a lot from Kaushy – who still oversees the roasting and grinding of their own special Garam Masala mix. The first dish Minal introduced to the menu was her Bara Kebab, which remains a firm favourite with customers today.

Bobby and Minal do not believe in shortcuts. They take their time to ensure perfection. With her sights set on fine dining, Minal has already created a menu which commands 2 AA rosettes and Prashad has been awarded a Michelin Bib Gourmand for the last few years. With TripAdvisor also awarding the restaurant a Certificate of Excellence for the last six years, they are no strangers to success and recognition for their hard work. Something of great importance to the team is making sure their success translates into wider benefits, and they do so with their own giving concept – Prashadam, organising an evening each month where all profits go to a nominated charity.

**Find them at:**

137 Whitehall Road, Drighlington, BD11 1AT
Tel: 0113 285 2037
Email: info@prashad.co.uk
**www.prashad.co.uk**

# PRITHVI
## CHELTENHAM

**No shorts, caps, flip-flops or children under 12 allowed, states the website of this upscale gem, located in Cheltenham. Opened in 2012 by Jay Rahman and Taj Uddin, Prithvi has gone from strength to strength as each year passes by..**

Prithvi translates as 'Mother Earth' in Sanskrit, and it was this that inspired the two to return to their roots and open a restaurant providing a mix of reinvented Indian and Bangladeshi dishes. As one of the few UK restaurants to have a full star rating on TripAdvisor, you can see for yourself why their customers keep coming back for more.

Prithvi pride themselves on their ability to reinvent Indian classics, and with a Bengali head chef and a pastry chef from France, the mix of cultures, flavours and textures are difficult to miss. With their pristine white tablecloths and sleek grey walls adorned with local artwork, Prithvi want to provide their customers with a comfortable, relaxed dining experience.

While at first glance their menu may appear to be rather on the simple side, Prithvi hold tricks up their sleeves at every turn, claiming that everything that seems ordinary is hiding a delightful twist.

Prithvi were named winners of the OpenTable 'Fit for Foodies' Award at the National Restaurant Awards in 2016 and are popular as ever today; if you're wanting to pay them a visit on a weekend break, make sure to call ahead

as they have been known to be fully booked for up to months in advance.

If you are already in the area and don't want to miss out on the opportunity to dine here, there is always the option of dropping by at lunch for one of their two or three-course set menus. If you're lucky enough to find yourself visiting for dinner, make sure you check out the Tour of Prithvi. With five courses costing £53, you'll be taken on a culinary adventure, experiencing a different range of flavours and spices at each course.

**Find them at:**
37 Bath Road, Cheltenham, GL53 7HG
Tel: 01242 226229
Email: info@prithvirestaurant.com
**prithvirestaurant.com**

# OX CHEEK & CARROTS WITH CLOVES

**Serves 4**

INGREDIENTS

1kg ox cheek
500g carrots, large
18 garlic cloves
2 tablespoons ginger, grated
2 large onions
100ml rapeseed oil/unrefined mustard oil
½ tablespoon salt
15 cloves
8 cardamom pods
2 cinnamon sticks
5 bay leaves
20 black peppercorns
¾ tablespoon curry powder
¾ tablespoon turmeric powder
¾ tablespoon cumin powder
¾ tablespoon coriander powder
¾ tablespoon paprika
Chilli powder, to taste
1 litre hot water
Fresh coriander

**As with all dishes at Prithvi, their Ox Cheek recipe dates back to the time when spices were first being discovered. Prithvi's Ox Cheeks are full of flavour and are even better when cooked slowly over a few hours – perfect for a lazy Sunday.**

Preheat the oven to 160°C.

Prepare the ox cheek by cutting it into large cubes.

Cut the carrots into chunks and set aside with the ox cheek.

Crush 18 garlic cloves under a large knife and grate a large piece of ginger (enough to fill 2 tablespoons). Slice the onions.

Add 100ml of rapeseed oil or unrefined mustard oil to a deep casserole dish and place over medium to low heat.

Add the crushed garlic and grated ginger to the dish and lightly brown.

Add the sliced onions, half a tablespoon of salt, cloves, cardamom, cinnamon sticks, bay leaves and black peppercorns. Stir lightly until the onions are lightly browned.

Reduce to a low heat, add the ox cheek and stir until brown.

# DAHI KE KEBAB

**Serves 4**

INGREDIENTS

4 tablespoons Hung or Greek yoghurt
1 large onion, chopped
2 green chillies, chopped
½ teaspoon ginger, chopped
1 tablespoon fresh coriander leaves, chopped
½ teaspoon black peppercorns
Salt, to taste
4 large potatoes
2 tablespoons cornflour
3 tablespoons plain flour
90g breadcrumbs
Oil, for frying

In a large mixing bowl, add the yoghurt, onion, chillies, ginger, coriander leaves, peppercorns and salt, mix well and set aside.

Boil the potatoes in a large saucepan. Once boiled, peel and grate the potatoes, then mash thoroughly.

Add salt and cornflour, mix well and divide into eight equal portions.

Stuff each portion with the yoghurt mixture, then shape into balls and flatten.

Add the plain flour to a clean mixing bowl, then add enough water to create a thin batter.

Dip the flattened balls in the batter, then coat in the breadcrumbs.

Heat the oil in a frying pan and deep fry the flattened balls until light golden brown.

Serve with mint chutney or ketchup.

# PUSHKAR

## BIRMINGHAM

**Bright, brilliant and bustling, you can't miss Pushkar. Sure, it helps that it sits proudly on Birmingham's golden mile. Ask any Brummie and they'll be able to direct you to Broad Street, without doubt the city's best-known thoroughfare.**

But Pushkar is about more than just a good location. It's a restaurant and cocktail bar par excellence – the bar is the place to be seen of a Friday night and as for the food... I well remember my first visit and being left stunned by the presentation alone. The hands-on owners are surprisingly modest about the Pushkar phenomenon, but it's fair to say our experience there bettered that of a recent visit to a central London Michelin-starred Indian restaurant.

Pushkar's menu is inspired by North Indian and Punjabi cuisine, and the restaurant's chefs want to continue pushing boundaries and challenging traditional methods with modern techniques, to create new flavours and experiences for their diners.

Diners are fast coming to associate more than just heat with Indian cuisine, appreciating that it's more about the nuances of the different spices and ingredients. It's a formula which has apparently made it the first stop for certain high-flyers returning to Blighty after jetting in from as far afield as New York and Dubai.

As for customer service, whether you dine in Pushkar's main restaurant, in their private dining room or in their

Lotus Room that can accommodate up to 75 guests, you'll receive the same high level of service from the front of house team.

The people at Pushkar believe 'when style meets substance' is their motto, and it would be a difficult task to find many who disagree.

**Find them at:**
245 Broad Street, Birmingham, B1 2HQ
Tel: 0121 643 7978
Email: dining@pushkardining.com
**www.pushkardining.com**

# ROMY'S KITCHEN

## BRISTOL

**Romy Gill is one of the few female Indian chef-owners in the UK, and her restaurant Romy's Kitchen has allowed her to showcase her talent for creating beautiful Indian dishes.**

In the five years since her debut on the restaurant scene in Thornbury, Bristol, Romy's Kitchen has become a magnet for visitors from far and wide who've come not only because they've heard about the menu, but because they've heard wonderful things about Romy.

Her formidable media profile is a far cry from her early life, born and brought up in West Bengal to a Punjabi family. As a child, her kitchen would be full of the smells and flavours of regions all across India. Today, the food at Romy's Kitchen reflects these influences, and her food is inspired by numerous regions across the subcontinent. Not only finding inspiration in the flavours and spices she grew up with, Romy enjoys experimenting with British ingredients, some of which she didn't even know existed until she moved to the UK.

The kitchen isn't the only place you'll find Romy, and if you've turned on your TV or read a newspaper in the last few years, chances are you'll have stumbled across her face, her voice or even her words. Romy regularly contributes to food publications and had a residency in The Guardian. In April 2016, she also appeared on Celebrity MasterChef and The Hairy Bikers Comfort Food series, and is a regular judge for the BBC Radio 4 Food and Farming Awards.

Despite her busy schedule, Romy's Kitchen isn't ever an afterthought, and the food and service you'll find here is of a high calibre. The hard work that Romy puts into everything she does has not gone unrecognised – she was awarded an MBE in the Queen's 90th birthday honours list in 2016, for services to the hospitality industry.

**Find them at:**

2 Castle Street, Thornbury, Bristol, BS35 1HB

Tel: 01454 416728

Email: eat@romyskitchen.co.uk

**www.romyskitchen.co.uk**

# BUTTER CHICKEN

**Serves 3-4**

INGREDIENTS

MARINADE

500g boneless chicken, diced
50g smooth Greek natural yoghurt
1 teaspoon ginger, finely grated
1 teaspoon garlic, finely grated
½ teaspoon garam masala
½ teaspoon tandoori masala
1 teaspoon cumin powder
1 teaspoon coriander powder
2 teaspoons red Kashmiri chilli powder

SAUCE

6 tablespoons cashew nuts
6 teaspoons ghee (or oil)
3 teaspoons ginger, finely grated
2 teaspoons garlic, finely grated
8 teaspoons tomato purée
3 teaspoons dried fenugreek leaves
½ teaspoon ground turmeric
1 teaspoon garam masala
1 teaspoon tandoori masala
2 teaspoons salt
1 teaspoon Kashmiri chillies
500ml single cream
400ml water

**Romy Gill remembers this dish fondly as it brings her back to her childhood and travelling from West Bengal to her grandparents' home in Punjab. Butter chicken is a rich and creamy dish that suits most tastebuds, and while you're already treating yourself, why not go all out and add some rice and breads on the side?.**

Mix together all marinade ingredients and marinate the chicken for a minimum of two hours (overnight if you've got the time).

Preheat the oven to 200°C.

Soak the cashew nuts in hot water for 10 minutes, drain and then grind into a fine paste in a blender, adding a little water if required.

Place the marinated chicken on a baking tray and cook for 10-12 minutes until the chicken is tender and cooked.

# AUNTY AJEET'S TANDOORI STYLE LAMB CHOPS

**Serves 4**

INGREDIENTS

2kg rack of lamb, cut into chops
Salt, to taste
Juice of 1 lemon
2 cloves garlic, crushed
½ tablespoon cumin powder
½ tablespoon coriander seeds
5 cloves
4 green cardamoms
15-20 whole black peppercorns
Pinch ginger powder
1 cinnamon stick
1 tablespoon paprika
¼ tablespoon chilli powder
¼ tablespoon cultured yoghurt
¼ tablespoon ginger and garlic paste

An old family recipe originating in North India, Aunty Ajeet's recipe can be served at any family get-together as it will be loved by all, old, young or in between. Aunty Ajeet's recipe uses lamb, but if you'd prefer, you can swap this out with a protein of your choice – chicken is a firm favourite of the family, and Sachins' customers!

Score each of the lamb chops with a knife and rub salt and the juice of one full lemon into it, then leave for 10 minutes to marinate.

Rub the garlic and ginger paste into the lamb chops and leave in the fridge to marinate for a further 30 minutes.

Grind all of the dried spices together, then mix them into the yoghurt along with the garlic and ginger paste.

Take the marinade and apply generously all over the lamb chops.

Leave the lamb in the fridge to marinate for at least 30 minutes, but preferably overnight.

Pre-heat the oven to 220°C.

Place the lamb on a metal grill tray and cook for 20-25 minutes, turning once and brushing with oil.

Finally, grill or barbecue the lamb to cook and taste.

# SACHINS

## NEWCASTLE-UPON-TYNE

**Located on the historic Forth Banks of Newcastle-upon-Tyne, Sachins has become known for the bold colours and flavours you'll find on its Punjabi-inspired menu.**

Kulmeet (Bob) Arora took over the 35-year-old restaurant in 2000 and 18 years on is still as passionate about the restaurant as ever. Many of the dishes on the menu at Sachins are family recipes that have been passed down from generation to generation, and with Bob acting as head chef as well as owner, he makes sure that all that he was taught by his family he is able to instil in his own chefs.

Originally only serving North Indian and Punjabi dishes, Sachins have recently branched out and become slightly more experimental when it comes to their menu, with Bob and his team starting to find excitement in South Indian food. Though they're careful not to stray too far from where they began. Bob says his motto is 'if it isn't broken, don't try and fix it', and he believes it's consistency that brings their regulars back to them time and time again. They take pride in the fact that at Sachins they are able to say that they can watch their customers grow from children to adults who go on to introduce their own children to the restaurant.

Sachins isn't popular only with Newcastle locals though. The team at Sachins are certain that if someone visits them from outside the area, they'll be sure to come back the next time they're in the city. Sachins continue to make lasting impressions on their customers, and they can even make their own little mark on your big day. They can cater for events and weddings, organising everything from music and entertainment, down to the cake.

**Find them at:**
Forth Banks, Newcastle-upon-Tyne, NE1 3SG
Tel: 0191 261 9035
Email: info@sachins.co.uk
**www.sachins.co.uk**

# SCENE INDIAN STREET KITCHEN

## MANCHESTER

**Scene Indian Street Kitchen was an exciting new addition to Manchester's Spinningfields district when it opened three years ago, and it remains just as exciting today as it did then.**

Wanting to set themselves apart from other, more traditional Indian restaurants, the Ali family opened Scene with the intentions of creating a fun, innovative, young and quirky restaurant that would offer their diners an experience they wouldn't be able to find elsewhere.

Before even getting to sit down and order from Scene's varied menu, customers are blown away by the visuals of the restaurant. Not your typical one room location with 20 tables, Scene spans five separate dining areas.

The restaurant has two separate outdoor spaces – The Veranda where customers can enjoy the restaurant's street food (and shisha is available for over 18s); and the Riverside Terrace, decorated with lanterns and furniture inspired by the subcontinent, described as the perfect place for customers to host their own private parties or barbecues.

Inside, the more modern main restaurant combines shack-style booths and Indian artefacts and antiques with artwork from local artists, while the Bollywood Bar serves customers traditional Indian lagers and specialised Indian signature cocktails and mocktails in 1950s inspired surroundings. Scene's semi-private VIP area overlooks the Riverside Terrace and the River Irwell, with enough space to comfortably seat 20 guests.

Once you've decided which part of the restaurant to get comfortable in, you'll find yourself with an even harder decision to make – what to choose from their extensive menu. Street food is Scene's main attraction, offering tapas-style Indian food inspired by different regions within India and Pakistan, with speciality mains and innovative dishes you won't find anywhere else.

Scene Indian Street Kitchen hold themselves to a very high standard when it comes to serving their customers the best, most authentic dishes, while still providing them with their own unique take on tradition. Open seven days a week, Scene welcome customers from all walks of life to join them and make them their home away from home, a place to go and celebrate or just to relax and enjoy their unique food and atmosphere.

**Find them at:**
4a Leftbank, Spinningfields, Manchester, M3 3AN
Tel: 0161 839 3929
**www.scenedining.com**

# FISH AMRITSARI

**Serves 3-4**

**INGREDIENTS**

**FISH AMRITSARI**

600g cod
Salt, to taste
2 tablespoons garlic paste
2 tablespoons ginger paste
¼ teaspoon black pepper
1 tablespoon lemon juice
120g gram flour
1 tablespoon red chilli powder
¼ teaspoon turmeric
1 tablespoon carom seeds
Oil, for frying

**GARNISH**

Chaat masala
Fresh ginger strands
Fresh coriander
Lemon wedges

Slice the fish into small, equal bite-size pieces.

Marinate the fish in the salt, garlic and ginger pastes, black pepper and lemon juice.

Set this aside for 15-20 minutes to let the fish marinate.

In a separate bowl, mix together the gram flour, red chilli powder, turmeric and carom seeds and add a small amount of water to form a thick batter.

Coat the fish pieces in the batter and leave to rest for 5 minutes.

Fry in hot oil until golden brown and crispy.

**Garnish**

Sprinkle with some chaat masala, fresh ginger and coriander and top with some fresh lemon wedges, squeezing a little over the fish just before serving.

# RAJASTHANI PAPAD KI SABZI

**Serves 4**

**INGREDIENTS**

40g ghee
4g cumin seeds
3g asafoetida
8g green chilli, chopped
35g ginger and garlic paste
5g coriander powder
3g red chilli powder
3g turmeric powder
270g red onion purée
250g fresh tomato purée
500ml water
200g natural yoghurt, whisked
1g kasuri methi (dried fenugreek leaves)
Salt, to taste
8 poppadums

**FOR THE TADKA**

5g ghee
1g fenugreek seeds
2 whole dried red chillies
7g garlic, roughly chopped

Rajasthani cooking has its own unique flavour, where the simplest and most basic ingredients come together to create the most innovative dishes. Originally created as a solution to vegetable shortages in this desert area during the summer, Rajasthani Papad Ki Sabzi was thought up by the women of the region who still wanted to cook something healthy, whether there were vegetables available or not.

Melt the ghee in a hot heavy-based pan. Cook the cumin and allow it to crackle.

Add the asafoetida, green chillies and the ginger and garlic paste and sauté for two to three minutes.

Sprinkle in the powdered spices, stir-fry quickly and then add the onion and tomato purées and cook for 10 minutes.

Pour in the water and cook for a further 10 minutes, then add the yoghurt and cook on a medium heat until the oil starts to separate.

Check the consistency of the sauce – it should resemble that of single cream – and finish with the dried fenugreek leaves (rub between your palms before you add them)

Put all ingredients for the tadka in a pan and stir until the garlic turns golden brown and then add to the sauce.

Cut the poppadums into quarters and add to the sauce – they should soften in under a minute.

Serve with Millet (Bajra) bread/roti.

# TALLI JOE
## LONDON

**Talli is the Hindi word for tipsy and happy. With a name like this, you can expect your experience at the restaurant to be one to remember – or maybe not? Their website describes the menu as one made up of 'half plates and full drinks'; tapas-style portions that allow customers to order and sample different flavours from regional India.**

Talli Joe is the brainchild of promoter Shilpi Gandhi Khutale. Unimpressed by the standard of Indian restaurants in London when she moved to the capital, she struggled to find the food that she had enjoyed back home. Everything Indian was made milder for the UK market, and Shilpi wanted to open a restaurant that would unleash a menu full of flavour and present diners with traditional local dishes as they are meant to be tasted.

Ever-growing international travel has only increased the appetite for authentic styles of cuisine, with travellers seeking to recreate the same dining experience after they return home. Talli Joe takes its inspiration from home cooks across various regions of India, drawing on the wisdom of mothers whose cooking styles are learned through generations handing down their family recipes.

With a smart Shaftesbury Avenue location, Talli Joe have already received critical acclaim and notched up a further success by winning the OpenTable Diners' Choice Award 2018.

**Find them at:**

152-156 Shaftesbury Avenue, London, WC2H 8HL

Tel: 020 7836 5400

Email: info@tallijoe.com

**www.tallijoe.com**

# THALI HO
## SURBITON

**Shamim and Shah Malek grew up in Surbiton and spent their childhoods helping out in the curry houses owned by their parents. Both brothers shared the dream of one day opening a contemporary Indian restaurant that would serve the recipes handed down to them by their parents and grandparents, and they've achieved this dream by opening Thali Ho.**

Their parents moved to Britain from Bangladesh in the 1970s and opened several successful restaurants. Good business sense must run in the Malek family as Thali Ho was awarded 'Best Casual Dining Restaurant in the London Suburbs' at the Asian Curry Awards 2017 within three weeks of opening their doors.

Thali Ho, as the name would suggest, focuses on Thali-style dining where customers are served a platter of items, each in their own small dishes called katoris. Shamim is the man behind the menu and believes that maintaining a relatively small menu is the key to success, as having a menu with hundreds of items for diners to choose from can put pressure on a restaurant and cause standards to slip. Shamim has instead created a smaller range of authentic dishes that use quality ingredients, and there definitely seems to be enough choice for Thali Ho's diners as they keep coming back for more.

The thali platters they serve here are a feast almost as much for the eye as they are for the tastebuds.

Thali Ho's interior is bright and modern, with exposed brick walls and hardwood floors. Their eye-catching turquoise exterior piques your interest and draws you in, and the bursts of colour continue inside the restaurant with their blue, red, green and yellow seating. Thali Ho has an instant laid-back feel to it, and you're sure to hear the sound of diners talking and laughing, creating an atmosphere that makes you want to return time and time again.

**Find them at:**

31-33 Brighton Road, Surbiton, KT6 5LR

Tel: 020 8399 0094 / 020 8399 4434

Email: info@thali-ho.co.uk

**www.thali-ho.co.uk**

# GOAN SEABASS CURRY

## SERVED WITH FLUFFY STEAMED RICE

**Serves 2**

**INGREDIENTS**
2 seabass fillets
Fresh coriander

**MARINADE**
1 teaspoon mustard oil
½ teaspoon cumin
½ teaspoon turmeric
½ teaspoon chilli powder
Salt, to taste

**SAUCE**
1 tablespoon mustard oil
1 teaspoon mustard seeds
1 bay leaf
1 medium onion, finely sliced
½ teaspoon cumin
½ teaspoon chilli powder
½ teaspoon turmeric
2 whole green chillies
½ teaspoon garam masala
1 fresh tomato
1 teaspoon salt, or to taste

One of Thali Ho's signature dishes, their Goan seabass curry has proved popular with their diners since their opening. The dish is rich in spices yet doesn't pack an overwhelming punch, and it's an easy one to put together at home. Chef and co-owner Shamim Malek suggests serving with fluffy steamed rice to enhance but not distract from the flavours, and using fresh, good quality seabass fillets, and descaling but leaving the skin on before cooking.

Add all ingredients for the marinade to a mixing bowl, then mix together to form a paste.

Rub the paste evenly on to the seabass fillets, then refrigerate for 30 minutes to absorb the marinade.

While the seabass is marinating in the paste, add the ingredients for the sauce into a large saucepan and stir frequently for about 30 minutes, or until the sauce is thick in consistency.

Remove the seabass from the fridge and shallow fry until cooked through.

Once cooked, add the seabass to the sauce, garnish with a generous amount of freshly chopped coriander, simmer, serve and enjoy.

THALI HO

# CHICKEN LOLLIPOPS

**Serves 4**

**INGREDIENTS**

6 large whole chicken wings
Approx. 750ml vegetable oil, for deep frying

**BATTER**

4 tablespoons corn flour
2 tablespoons flour
2 tablespoons rice flour
½ tablespoon red chilli powder
¼ tablespoon ground black pepper
¼ tablespoon white pepper powder
¼ tablespoon garlic powder
½ tablespoon chicken stock
¼ tablespoon salt (or to taste)
1 whole egg
Approx. 50/75ml water

**MARINADE**

1 tablespoon ginger paste
1 tablespoon garlic paste
½ tablespoon salt
½ tablespoon freshly ground black pepper
1 tablespoon light soy sauce
Juice from half a lemon

One of their signature must-have dishes, Tuk Tuk Indian's Chicken Lollipops are known for their unique lollipop shape that comes from using the 'frenching' technique (head to your local butchers and ask them to prepare your wings for you). These artfully crafted chicken wings are marinated, dipped in a spiced batter and then deep-fried, making them deliciously crispy to bite into. Tuk Tuk Indian serve these up with their house tamarind and tempered tomato sauce, but you can pair them with any dip of your choice.

Rinse the wings with cold water and leave to drain in a colander.

Mix all of your marinade ingredients in a large bowl.

Add the chicken wings to the marinade and leave to rest for at least 30-45 minutes.

Add the batter ingredients into a large bowl and mix well. Add a little water at a time until you have a slightly thick batter.

Prepare the oil for frying in either a shallow frying pan or an electrical deep fat fryer, bringing the temperature to 160°C.

Roll the meat end of the chicken into a lollipop shape, then dip into the batter.

Once the oil is ready, place the lollipops (one at a time) into the hot oil and fry for approximately 5 minutes, ensuring they have cooked through and are golden brown and crispy on the outside.

Remove the lollipops from the oil and drain on a plate with some kitchen towel

Serve hot with a dip of your choice.

# TUK TUK INDIAN

## EDINBURGH, GLASGOW

**Anyone who has travelled by rail in India cannot fail to be struck by the sights and sounds of the railway station. Not least among them are the ever-present food hawkers, who ply their trade among the noise and bustle.**

Tuk Tuk Indian are seeking to recreate at least part of the experience, surprising customers with the flavours they serve up in their Edinburgh and Glasgow restaurants. Their menu boasts a mixture of rustic roadside and classic Indian railway station dishes, each one packing a punch, despite the relatively small size of the plates.

The chefs at Tuk Tuk Indian hail from all walks of life and countless different regions of Asia and the subcontinent; from Mumbai and Delhi to Nepal and Bangladesh, these chefs work together to create a menu that displays the best of each region and stays as true to the recipes they grew up with as possible. With the standard of Indian cuisine in the UK increasing day by day, the team at Tuk Tuk aren't shying away from the competition they face, nor are they changing themselves or their menu to appeal to a wider audience.

If you like your curry hot, this place is for you. Tuk Tuk refuse to water down anything they serve. They remain adamant they will continue to serve only the best and the most genuine Indian dishes, not removing any ingredient that would be used back in India in favour of something more often found in the UK. This has had the unexpected effect of making Tuk Tuk a favourite with holidaymakers from India, who dine with them knowing the flavours will make them feel right at home, even when they're thousands of miles away.

Tuk Tuk's success was recognised with the Best Scottish Street Food Award. Now the people behind it plan to one day see a series of Tuk Tuks dotted across the UK – so this is certainly not the end of the line!

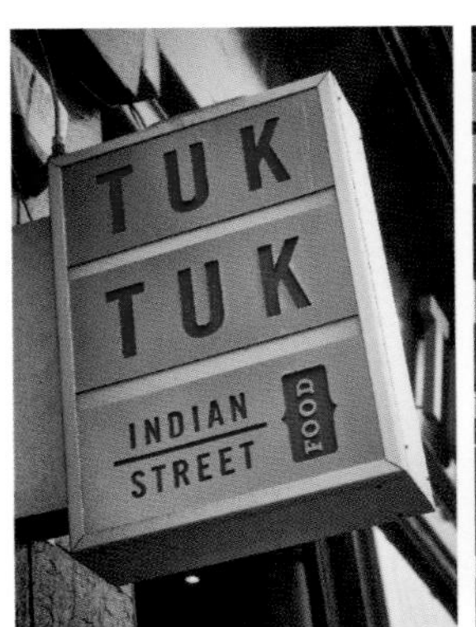

**Find them at:**
1 Leven Street, Edinburgh, EH3 9LH
Tel: 0131 228 3322
Email: infowallah@tuktukonline.com

426 Sauchiehall Street, Glasgow, G2 3JD
Tel: 0141 332 2126
Email: glasgow@tuktukonline.com

**www.tuktukonline.com**

# THE VALLEY

## NORTH EAST ENGLAND

**Full steam ahead!**
**With venues across the North East of England, the Valley restaurants have made a name for themselves as more than just places to eat – because they're your ticket to a unique dining experience.**

And it's one that has customers arriving by the trainload. From its base at the Old Station House in Corbridge, The Valley Corbridge was the first of the three restaurants to open, doing so in February 1991, and quickly made its mark among those who like to arrive in style.

The Valley's Passage to India 'Curry Train' service escorts pre-booked customers from Newcastle Central Station straight to the restaurant's doors. With uniformed staff, drinks and menus on board, the experience evokes memories of a grand age of travel. Upon arrival, diners are treated to a five-course meal before their return journey back into the city.

The Valley Junction 397 and The Valley Connection 301 (the numbers correspond to the dates in which they opened, March 1997 and March 2001), follow suit when it comes to original locations, with the former in a train carriage and signal box at the Old Station in Jesmond and the latter in the historic market place of Hexham, overlooking its stunning abbey.

The menu at The Valley does well to match up to their singular locations, with owner Daraz and brother Locku

creating a refined menu which they have adapted to the tastes of their customers. With influences from across the subcontinent, their main theme originates from Sylhet, the North-East region of Bangladesh.

Daraz and Locku believe that Indian cuisine is developing, and are leaving room for the next generation of the family to make an impact, starting with the opening of Cilantro – a new Indo-Latino tapas bar in the heart of Newcastle.

**Find them at:**

The Valley Corbridge Limited
Old Station House, Station Road, Corbridge, NE45 5AY
Tel: 01434 633434

The Valley Junction 397
The Old Station, Jesmond Three Sixty,
Newcastle upon Tyne, NE2 1DB
Tel: 0191 281 6397

The Valley Connection
T/A The Valley in the City Limited, 19 Market Place,
Hexham, NE46 3NX
Tel: 01434 601234

**www.valleyrestaurants.co.uk**

# BHUNA GOSHT

**Serves 2**

**INGREDIENTS**

2 tablespoons oil
2 medium onions, finely chopped
1 teaspoon salt
1 tablespoon garlic paste
1 tablespoon ginger paste
1 teaspoon cumin powder
½ teaspoon coriander powder
1 teaspoon chilli powder
½ teaspoon turmeric powder
225g lamb or beef, diced
3 bay leaves
3 cardamom pods
1 cinnamon stick
Fresh coriander, chopped, to garnish
2 green chillies, chopped
1 teaspoon garam masala

**This rich and spicy meat dish is a favourite across all of The Valley restaurants. With subtle influences from across the subcontinent, the dish is full of flavours that will leave you struggling to put down your fork.**

Heat the oil in a pan over a low heat for a minute.

Add the onion into the pan, then add the salt and let simmer until the onions soften.

Add the garlic and ginger pastes and stir, then let simmer for 5 minutes.

Add the cumin, coriander powder, chilli powder, turmeric and stir. Add a little water if needed to stop the sauce from sticking to the pan.

Let the sauce simmer over a medium heat for 5 minutes to allow the spices to come together.

Add the beef or lamb to the thickened bhuna sauce.

Let the meat cook in the sauce 10 ten minutes.

Add the bay leaves, cardamom, cinnamon stick, half of the fresh coriander and one of the chopped chillies and stir into the curry, then let simmer for a further 5 minutes.

Finally, garnish with the remaining fresh coriander and green chilli, then serve and enjoy.

# VENISON
## WITH WILD MUSHROOM & ROCK MOSS SAUCE

**Game was a big part of the food scene in colonial India, and Varanasi wanted to introduce a dish that would reflect their fine dining status while holding on to elements of traditional Indian cuisine. Having taken inspiration from Michelin star restaurants in London, the chefs at Varanasi have developed this dish, which has fast become one of their favourites, just as it has their customers'.**

**Serves 4**

**INGREDIENTS**

4 x 180g venison fillets
20ml sunflower oil
5g coarse ground black pepper
4 pinches sea salt
200g wild mushrooms
100g baby spinach
1 tablespoon garlic, chopped
75g unsalted butter
1 teaspoon salt
1 teaspoon turmeric powder

**SAUCE**

250g onions, sliced
100ml Greek yoghurt
1 tablespoon garlic and ginger paste
6 cloves
1 cinnamon stick (4 inch)
1 teaspoon rock moss
1 teaspoon Degi chilli
1 teaspoon coriander powder
1 teaspoon garam masala
100ml venison glaze

Preheat the oven to 180°C.

Heat a frying pan and when hot add the sunflower oil.

Season the venison with salt and pepper and add to the pan and sear all sides of the fillets.

Place the venison on a baking sheet and place in the oven, roast for 40-45 minutes.

Once cooked, remove from the oven and wrap the fillets in foil, leaving to rest for at least 20 minutes to ensure that the meat is tender and perfectly cooked.

While the meat is resting, heat a saucepan and add the whole spices.

Add the onion until it starts to brown and then add the ginger and garlic paste and stir for 5 minutes.

Add the ground spices and the yoghurt and cook until the oil begins to separate and then blend until smooth.

Serve.

# VARANASI

## BIRMINGHAM

**It has an interior designed to rival the luxury restaurants of Dubai. It's the largest restaurant in its home city, occupying 2200 square feet and comfortably seating 350 customers over its three floors. Their four grand private dining rooms reflect the kind of opulence that can't be found without jumping on a 12-hour flight.**

It boasts three cocktails bars and has a whole page of the drinks menu dedicated to champagne.

Got it yet? We're of course referring to Varanasi, open barely a year but certainly making an impact from its lavish home on Broad Street, Birmingham.

Before opening, Varanasi's owner Mo travelled to India, Thailand, Dubai and China, researching their finest bars and restaurants to draw inspiration for both the look of his restaurant and most importantly, for the menu. The things he saw and learned on his travels helped to create the fine dining menu on offer at Varanasi today. Each day Varanasi's chefs – all of whom have worked at Michelin star restaurants in London – grind all of their spices fresh in-house, and there's no trace of any ready-made base curries in the kitchen here. Inspired by Punjabi cooking with elements of South Indian and Nepalese cuisine making appearances, Varanasi pride themselves on the high standard of food they serve.

In an environment where Indian cuisine across the UK is considered to be improving generally, Varanasi believe that

they have set the bar even higher for the Midlands. Their Black Card loyalty scheme, and the imminent launch of their chauffeur service will only reinforce their place up there with the very best, and perhaps even move them closer to their goal of one day being winning a coveted star in the Michelin Guide.

**Find them at:**

184 Broad Street, Birmingham B15 1DA
Tel: 0121 633 3700
Email: reservations@varanasi.uk
**www.varanasi.uk**

# ZOUK

## MANCHESTER, BRADFORD

**Brothers Tayub and Mudassar Amjad started Zouk with the modest but laudable aim of sharing authentic Pakistani and Indian cuisine with a modern twist, in comfortable, contemporary surroundings. But soon they were thinking bigger.**

They opened the first Zouk branch in Bradford in 2006, in the Leeds Road area which is now a central hub for authentic Indian and Pakistani food. This was followed by the opening of their Manchester flagship branch in 2009, a 300-cover restaurant featuring a state-of-the-art all-weather terrace and a mezzanine floor for parties and functions.

Each brother brings something different to the restaurant. Tayub is the business brains and Mudassar the passionate and energetic foodie. They both firmly believe in Zouk's ability to change the way diners see Indian cuisine and work closely with their chefs to keep the menu fresh and exciting.

Zouk is particularly keen to promote healthy options. The brothers want to rid Indian food of the stigma of not being good for you or merely a naughty treat. Zouk's menu features seafood, steaks, and a wide range of grilled dishes, with many of their curries being stir-fried in karahis.

Tayub and Mudassar's father was born in Lahore, Pakistan, where arguably some of the best street food in the world can be found. Zouk's menu features many classic dishes inspired by this city, such as their Samosa Chaat and their Lamb Nihari, and classic Karahis and Handis. Rather than

the limit the menu to this one region though, they also feature dishes such as Delhi's famous Chilli Paneer, the delicious classic Goan Fish Curry and Rajasthani-style Railway Lamb Curry.

The Amjad brothers would like to expand the brand both in the UK and abroad in the near future, but in the meantime they're focused on sharing their food discoveries with their customers and serving up the tastiest curries they can in Bradford and Manchester.

**Find them at:**
1312 Leeds Road, Bradford, BD3 8LF
Tel: 01274 258 025
Email: info@zoukteabar.co.uk

Unit 5, Chester Street, Manchester, M1 5QS
Tel: 0161 233 1090
Email: manchestermanager@zoukteabar.co.uk
**www.zoukteabar.co.uk**

# LOBSTER GWADRI KHAS

**Serves 1**

**INGREDIENTS**

1 whole lobster
½ yellow pepper, diced
½ red pepper, diced
½ red onion, diced
2 cloves garlic, diced
½ teaspoon salt
½ teaspoon turmeric
½ teaspoon chilli flakes
1 green chilli, chopped
½ teaspoon ground cumin
½ teaspoon paprika
3 teaspoons vegetable oil
Coriander, to garnish

**This dish is a real celebration of flavour and relies on quality ingredients to create a show-stopping dish. As Zouk specialises in seafood, they've created this stunning masala lobster dish, prepared with gentle spices. The spices used here bring out the flavours of the seafood rather than overpowering it. Serve as part of a luxurious banquet or as the main course for special occasions, especially when presented in the lobster shell as this makes it a great centrepiece on any table.**

Bring a large pan of water to the boil and add the lobster, then boil for 10 minutes.

Once boiled, drain the water and remove the lobster, then cut lengthways down the centre, remove the meat and wash the cavity out under running water.

Dice the meat that has been removed.

In a separate pan, place the empty lobster shell in warm water on a low heat to keep warm.

Add the oil to a hot pan, then add the peppers, onion and garlic and sauté until the onions turn brown and then add all of the spices and cook for 30 seconds.

Add a cup of water and turn the heat to low to simmer.

Once the mixture has been reduced by half, add the diced lobster meat and cook for a further 10 minutes.

Remove the lobster from the warm water and dry.

Place the lobster on a plate and add the mixture of the meat/peppers/spices into the lobster.

Garnish with coriander and serve with basmati rice.

# KING PRAWN PIRO PIRO

## SERVED WITH AN APPLE, KIWI AND CELERY SALAD

**INGREDIENTS**

16 king prawns
4 tablespoons sunflower oil
1 teaspoon lemon juice
1 teaspoon freshly ground black pepper
16 fresh curry leaves, finely chopped
1 green chilli, finely chopped
1 teaspoon fine rice flour
4 garlic cloves, finely chopped
1 inch ginger, finely chopped
2 teaspoon Kashmiri chilli powder or ½ teaspoon paprika and ½ teaspoon chilli powder
1 teaspoon turmeric powder
1 tablespoon vinegar
1 teaspoon black salt (or sea salt), to taste

**Chef Binod's signature dish fits perfectly within Zumbura's 'Light, Fresh and Healthy' ethos. This plate doesn't take too long to whip up, but that doesn't mean it's lacking in flavour.**

Combine all ingredients (except prawns) to make a paste.

Marinate the prawns in the paste for 20 minutes.

Place the prawns on a grill, meat side down, until grill marks appear.

Turn the prawns over so that they're skin side down and grill until they turn a vibrant red.

Serve on a bed of apple, kiwi and celery salad.

# ZUMBURA

## LONDON

**The bright chairs and tables positioned outside the restaurant may well be what captures the attention of Zumbura's walk-in customers. But it's the food, drink and the atmosphere inside the restaurant that get people visiting from all over the country. Chef-patron Binod Baral wants Zumbura to be seen as a destination – if he is willing to travel 50 miles to try a new dish, why shouldn't others?**

Inside, the wooden bar, brick walls and exposed light fixtures may look basic, but then you don't come to Zumbura to contemplate interior design. A better bet is home-style cooking inspired by the Purab region of North India. Zumbura's mantra is 'Light, Fresh & Healthy'; and unusually for an Indian restaurant, Zumbura use no cream or butter in the dishes. Baral assures us that nothing is put on the menu here if it doesn't have a story behind it. Zumbura is worth checking out for its cocktails alone. Indulge in a range of Indian themed cocktails, topped by the intriguing Zumbura Number 1 – an unlikely mix of Turmeric-infused East London Gin, Pimms, green cardamom, Fever Tree tonic and cinnamon. But it works!

It only takes one short conversation with Baral to know just how passionate he is about the culinary world. Binod first became a Head Chef at the age of 20 and in 2003, soon graduating to being appointed the youngest ever Group Executive Head Chef at the Bombay Bicycle Club, the largest chain of Indian restaurants outside of India. Working alongside Binod is Executive Chef Raju Rawat, a man with more than two decades of experience behind him. Trained at one of the finest five-star hotel groups in India, Raju went on to work at Michelin star restaurant Benares in Mayfair before helping to develop the popular street food brand Moolis, and then joining the team at Zumbura.

**Find them at:**
36a Old Town, Clapham, London SW4 0LB
Tel: 0207 720 7902
Email: info@zumbura.com
**zumbura.com**